S0-DPF-159

Journey to Wholeness

By:
Dennean Handfield

To ~~[redacted]~~,
Thank you for your
support. I hope you
enjoy.
love
Dennean

GP
GODZCHILD PUBLICATIONS

Copyright @ 2013 by Dennean Handfield

Published by Godzchild Publications
a division of Godzchild, Inc.
22 Halleck St., Newark, NJ 07104
www.godzchildproductions.net

Printed in the United States of America 2013—First Edition

All rights reserved. Except as permitted under the U.S. Copyright Act of 1976, this publication shall not be broadcast, rewritten, distributed, or transmitted, electronically or copied, in any form, or stored in a database or retrieval system, without prior written permission from the author.

Library of Congress Cataloging-in-Publications Data
Journey to Wholeness / Dennean Handfield

ISBN 978-1-937095-89-5

THE HOLY BIBLE, NEW INTERNATIONAL VERSION®, NIV® Copyright © 1973, 1978, 1984, 2011 by Biblica, Inc.® Used by permission. All rights reserved worldwide.

TABLE OF CONTENTS

—⁂—

ACKNOWLEDGEMENTS

It has been a dream come true in completing my first book. This would not be possible if it wasn't for God who gave me the vision for *Journey to Wholeness.* Thank you to my mom, whose love that has shaped me into the woman I am today; thank you for your constant prayers and believing in my dreams. Your love is a true reflection of God's love for me. My grandmom, Dee-Dee, your sweet loving spirit is nourishment to my soul. Thank you for being a part of my journey to womanhood and teaching me how to be classy without saying a word. My dad who continues to plant seeds of greatness in me. Your work ethic makes me strive to succeed, and your lesson on loving myself has been your greatest gift. To my pop, a.k.a. Mr. Marvin, your love for me is overwhelming; I am blessed to have you in my life. Thank you for being excited about this book. To my brother, Jay, who inspires me to be excellent in all things, you are a true reflection of strength. Our many talks helped me to strive for greatness. I love you. To my cousin, Monica, you always have seen greatness in me when I didn't see it in myself; thank you for reading and being an example that dreams do come true. My cousin, Courtnee, who read the first few pages and laughed at the characters, thank you for keeping my dream alive. To my cousin, Charrisse, thanks for all of the talks we had and your constant love and support. Thanks to my cousin, Corey and Stacie, for your inspiration and your encouraging words. To my sister, Cleta, who was one of the first readers, your excitement over the characters in this book inspired me to finish. Thank you for your input. To my angels Nevaeh, Alexis, CJ, and Jonathan...may all of dreams come true.

To the crew who has shown support and love when it was

only a dream.

My dear friend, Salimah Abdul, thank you for your constant support.

To Jamal, thank you for being my biggest cheerleader. Thank you for believing in me.

To Xavia Hobson, you were also a part of this journey. I will never forget when your mom told me how much you enjoyed reading it.

My publisher, Godzchild, Shaun and Ana Saunders, thank you both for your words of encouragement and this amazing opportunity. I am excited to be a part of the Godzchild family.

My editor, Michael DePasquale, thank you for your prayers and scriptures. I was excited that you saw the vision of what this book could do in the lives of young women.

Many thanks to Sir Anthony Spease, who has built my website to help spread the word about *Journey to Wholeness*, thank you for all that you do behind the scenes. It is much appreciated.

Many thanks to all who were a part of this journey and asked about the book. I can finally say it is finished.

I hope this book is an inspiration to young ladies to love themselves. Never settle for less.

DEDICATION

This book is dedicated in loving memory to my Pop-Pop, John T. Fields. Your resilient spirit and love continues to live in me.

May you rest in peace.

CHAPTER 1

Finally, the first day of my senior year, graduation couldn't come fast enough. These girls get on my last nerves. I hear them whisper every time I walk the halls. They call me every name in the book. I don't care, I'm going somewhere in my life, all I keep telling myself is to ignore them. Believe me it's hard; I would love to punch one of them dead in their face. Of course I won't, I need to watch out for this face. I'm not conceited, but I make heads turn. I feel them stare when I walk into a room. I must have something these girls want. I only wish I could see in myself what they see in me.

CHAPTER 2

"Patrice Johnson, get up," my mom screamed from the bottom of the stairs. "It's time to go to school. Just because you have a car doesn't mean you can get up whenever you want!"

"I'm up!" On my way to the bathroom, Kim, my best friend, texted me: *We're Seniors!!!!* That text alone gave me a burst of energy. I couldn't wait to get to school and spend time with her. I knew exactly what I was going to wear on the first day. My style is very classy and edgy. I love to wear heels. You would never catch me dead in sneakers. I pulled out a pair of black skinny jeans, black spiked stilettos and a pink t-shirt with a splash of silver accessories. My hair is jet black and I like wearing it out, letting the curls go wild. To complete my look I fluffed up hair and sprayed on my favorite Dior perfume and applied Mac lip gloss.

"If I call you one more time," my mom said from outside the room. "Your brother is riding with you!"

"I'm coming, Mom! Come on, big head." My younger brother, Desmond, is the perfect chocolate complexion you will ever see, and will definitely be a ladies man in his time.

Parking at McHenry High was always the worst, especially on the first day of school. My grandfather bought me a black Acura for my sixteenth birthday. As I walked the halls I noticed everyone in their new clothes. My best friend, Kim, was looking nice as usual, posted up against her locker, wearing a cropped black blazer with a with t-shirt and knee length jean shorts and red spiked heels. She was petite with silky black hair and light brown eyes.

"Patrice, over here," said Kim. I ran up to her as if I hadn't seen her in years. Her smile was always so bright and full of life. "Why didn't you reply to my text this morning?"

"I was rushing to get here. Can you believe we're seniors?" We both screamed, which got all of the other seniors joining in on the fun.

"Patrice, we are going to have so much fun this year. First thing is applying to NYU like we always dreamed of since we were little girls. Then we'll both shop for our prom dresses, then graduation. I am so happy!"

"Yeah, this year will be the best!" My smile was so big. Talking about our dreams made me so excited.

"Well, I will be trying out for cheerleading after school. It's something I've always wanted to try. And besides, you know I have the moves." Kim danced in the hall and guys banged a beat on their lockers. She popped her shoulders and head to the beat, everyone gathered around and screamed her name. My best friend was popular, and everyone loved her. I was sure she would make the cheerleading squad.

"Okay," I said. "Call me after the audition." Being late on the first day made me nervous.

"Promise. Talk to you later. Wish me luck." I sprinted to homeroom and heard my name.

"Yo, Patrice." It was Michael. I have been dating him on and off. "Why didn't you call me last night?"

"I was busy." He caressed my skin and leaned in to kiss me. I could have died happy right then and there.

"I thought you would never be too busy for me."

"You know I'm just playing. I was spending time with family last night. I always have time for you."

"Well, tonight is our night. Wait for me after school. We can catch a movie or something."

"Okay." I often felt like I was settling for Mike. That he only paid me attention at his convenience.

Time flew by in school. The final bell rang and everybody rushed to get home. I was glad my brother was going to walk home from school with friends; that would give me some time alone with Mike. I searched the hallways for him and found him at his locker, cornered by another girl. Tracy. She shoots slurs at me any time she could and always wanted what was mine, even my man. She was no beauty queen, but her body was fierce.

"Michael!" I said. "Are you ready?"

"Yeah, I'll be there in a minute." My heart dropped when he uttered those words. My body radiated and my hands dripped with sweat. What was I supposed to do? Should I have grabbed my man, and tell Tracy to find her own? Or should I have walked away in shame? No. I stood there, and waited patiently until he was done. I didn't even interrupt their flirtatious encounter.

"My fault babe. Tracy was giving me the notes from math class. I slept through the whole thing. We're having a test at the end of week."

"That's cool. What movie did you want to see?"

"I don't know. You pick." The line at the movies was long. I chose to see *The Fast & the Furious 6*. After the movie I was tired and took Mike home. He stayed with his grandmother at times because his relationship with his mom wasn't the greatest.

"I will call you tomorrow. I had fun tonight."

"Me too. I will see you in school tomorrow." As I drove home I thought about my relationship with Mike and how different he was acting. I couldn't put my finger on it, but I was sure it would eventually come out.

The next day in school Kim was waiting at my locker.

"I called you, and sent you about five text messages last night. Where were you?"

"Mike and I went to the movies, and I went straight to bed afterwards."

"Patrice, why do you keep seeing him, I don't think he's good for you."

"You are always quick to judge somebody. You don't even know Mike. He's been nothing but nice to you." Deep down I knew he wasn't any good, but I just felt the need to defend him.

"Patrice, I didn't want to tell you like this but the rumor is that he's been seen around with Tracy." I couldn't believe my ears. That is why he was acting so distant.

"I'm not trying to ruin your day about this. I'm your friend. I just don't want to see you get hurt." All I could do was stare at her, unsure of what to say. She probably noticed I was speechless, so she tried to lighten up the mood.

"Guess who made the cheerleading squad? Your girl did."

"Congratulations! I'm so happy for you. When is the first game?"

"Tomorrow. I actually have practice after school. Tiffany, Amber, and Lisa are coming to the game. You should sit with them."

"Alright, Miss Cheerleader. I can't wait."

Everyone in school the next day was excited for the first football game of the year. The cheerleaders wore their new uniforms. I didn't see Kim too much between classes, and didn't even see Mike during lunch period. After school I went to my first meeting to write for the school newspaper. I was also a member of student council and the yearbook committee.

The day seemed to fly by so instead of going home I waited after school for Kim's friends: Tiffany, Amber, and Lisa. They had been friends since elementary school. All three girls were fashionable and were fun to be with. Tiffany was one of those girls that had everything. Her dad was a well known minister, and her mom sold million dollar homes. She would come to school with the latest designer clothes, but never seemed stuck up. She was always very nice, and Kim liked her a lot. She was the only girl in school that had a Range Rover. A lot of the girls were jealous, but it never seemed to bother her, she stuck close to her friends, Lisa and Amber, whose parents were rich in their own right. Lisa's father was a judge, and her mother had her own PR firm. Amber's father was an engineer, and her mother was a clothing designer featured at New York's fashion week.

Tiffany walked towards me as if she was on a runway in Paris. She looked like a model, like she just stepped out of a magazine. Her skin was flawless, and she had a short haircut.
"Hey, Patrice, are you ready for the game?"

"I can't wait to cheer for my boyfriend and best friend."

"Well, let's go get a seat before it gets too crowded. You

know Kim wants us sitting front row."

As we waited for the game we talked about colleges, prom, and graduation. I looked forward to spending more time with the girls this year. We had so much in common. The crowd packed in the bleachers, the cheerleaders ran out to get the crowd ready for the game. They were doing back flips; Kim jumped up and landed in a split. She was so happy doing what she loved. The game started and I was the loudest one screaming for Mike to get the ball. Tracy was a couple of bleachers away, and I thought about what Kim told me, but pushed that thought away as simple gossip. After the game, we all stayed for the after party to celebrate McHenry High's first win. Mike and I danced to a few songs. Kim and her new cheerleading squad even did a few cheers amidst the roaring crowd. Even though everyone smiled around me, I felt so empty on the inside, but didn't know why. I didn't want to look sad, so I faked a smile.

With all of the excitement over the weekend, I failed to notice it was already Sunday. I never used to like going to church when I was a kid. I remember ripping holes in my stockings to stay home. My mom would threaten me: "No church; no play." Since I had gotten older, I looked forward to going. God always managed to talk directly to me. I threw on a simple black dress and black stilettos. My red Coach bag splashed a bit of color to the outfit. When I walked into the kitchen, my mom decided to start with me, of all days.

"I guess the dead decided to rise."

"Well, why didn't you come in, and check on me," I snapped.

"Patrice," said Desmond. He was sitting at the table like the perfect child. "Mom's just playing, have a little sense of humor."

I hated when my brother got in the middle of our altercations. It was his way of being the man of the house. My parents divorced when I was seven years old. Mom had said, "Your dad's not coming back." Just like that my dad was gone. I knew then my life would never be the same.

Church was as packed as always at Spirit and Truth. I grew up in this church. Every Sunday was like a family reunion. Of course,

I would hear things like, "Patrice, is that you?" "You got so big." "You look just like your mother." And I would just stand there and smile. Other girls just looked at me, and threw their noses up in the air. I never got how people could be so unfriendly in church. I made my way up to the front to get a good seat. I always wanted to be near the pastor. It made me feel closer to God. The choir started the service out strong. They sang my favorite song, "Rain on Me, Jesus." Tears rolled down my cheeks. I even threw up my hands. This is what people meant about feeling the Holy Spirit. After the choir, the pastor asked the congregation to open their Bibles and turn to Matthew 9. He preached about the woman with the issue of blood, how the whole town treated her like an outcast. When the woman heard about Jesus, she had faith that if she could touch his garb she would be healed. I thought that was such a powerful message. I've been looking for love in all the wrong places, all I needed was Jesus. The only problem was I didn't know how to reach Him.

After church I decided to call Mike. He didn't call me all day on Saturday. It was strange, but I figured he was just busy.

"Hey, what's up baby," he said.

"Are you just waking up? It's 3:00 in the afternoon."

"No, I'm just sitting here watching the game." He was distant for some reason. I just pushed those feelings aside.

"Do you want to do something later? I can come over and bring a movie."

"No, that's cool, baby. I have that math test tomorrow. I am going to catch up on some studying, and call it an early night. Can I make it up to you?"

"I guess. Call me after you're finished studying. Talk to you later."

"Okay, babe."

I couldn't believe we hung up like that. I kept telling myself to calm down. Maybe I should have gone there and saw what was really going on. Was Tracy there? While I was lost in my thoughts, I heard my name being screamed from downstairs. "Patrice! Come down, you've got company." I sprinted downstairs; it was Kim in the doorway. I wanted to hug her. She made me feel so much better.

"Hey, girl, I just thought I would stop by. I was wondering if you wanted to go to the mall or something."

"Yeah, just let me grab my coat. I can't wait to tell you what Mike did. Ugh."

Instead of going to the mall, Kim and I just drove around. We talked about going to NYU next fall. We had good grades in school, and she was involved in a lot of activities, which would look great on her application. I was very active in the school's news reporting. I told her how Mike was acting funny, how all of a sudden he had no time for me. She told me how Tracy had been hanging out with him after school for a while, but she didn't know how to tell me. I couldn't believe what I was hearing. Mike was more than a boyfriend. He was like a best friend. I couldn't believe he would betray me. I wanted to drive over his house, but Kim talked me out of it. I'm glad she did because God only knows what would have happened. She dropped me off. It was after 10:00 p.m. We laughed so hard. Those times we spent together reminded me why we were best friends.

I went straight to my room. I couldn't stop thinking about Mike. Even though Kim told me about his unfaithfulness, I still loved him. I wanted to pick up the phone, but my pride wouldn't let me do it. I just planned to talk to him in person at school. The moment my head hit the pillow, I was awakened by the phone.

"Hello." It was Mike.

"Hey, babe." I turned on the light to see the time and the clock read 2:00 a.m. The nerve of this fool calling me this time of morning.

"What's up, baby?"

"Is everything all right?"

"Yeah, I just pulled an all nighter. I think I'm ready for my test tomorrow. Sorry, to call you so late. I just wanted to hear your voice."

"Well, thanks for calling, but I don't have too much to say to you. You've been acting really distant lately."

"What! Come on, why are you acting like that. This is my senior year, and you know I'm on the basketball team. If coach sees me failing, I'm off the team and I would lose my scholarship. Why can't you be more understanding? How about I make it up to you? Let me take you out to dinner this weekend. You know I just want to see you happy. I love you." Those three words meant the world to me. Even if it was lie, I just wanted to believe that it was true. I knew I shouldn't have fallen too hard for Mike. There was definitely something going on between him and Tracy. But I also didn't want to let go until I found out the truth for myself.

"Yes, dinner this weekend sounds great."

CHAPTER 3

—ᴍ—

The school week flew by. All I could think about was the dinner date. Tracy and her friends glared at me, but I did what I do best: ignore them. I wasn't going to let her phase me. Mike was taking me out to dinner.

We went to a fancy Italian restaurant. There were white tablecloths on every table and candles burning in the middle. There was even a salt-water fish tank with beautiful, colorful fish that took up an entire wall. Mike pulled out my seat. He was great! We dated for over a year, and this was our first fancy dinner. He had something to prove.

"So what do you think? Did I outdo myself or what?"

"Yeah, baby. This place is nice. Everybody is so dressed up."

"I told you before, that all I want to do is make you happy. You need to start getting used to this treatment. Especially after I make it to the NBA! This is going to be our lifestyle!" We both laughed. It was always fun talking about our future together. Mike liked telling me how he was going to spoil me once he made it to the NBA. It wasn't a far-fetched dream for him. He stayed in the newspapers, and he was getting letters from colleges from all over the country.

"Yeah, I can't wait for you to spoil me." That statement felt like fantasy. For some reason, I knew that Mike was only in my life temporarily.

Mike and I talked and laughed until our stomachs hurt. The waiter came by with our menus. I couldn't even pronounce the choices. I decided to get the seafood linguini and a glass of raspberry iced tea. Mike stuck with the old-fashioned spaghetti and meatballs.

"Patrice, have I ever told you how beautiful you are? I always thought that the moment I saw you. I am not just saying that. These are the things that I've always wanted to do, but basketball always keeps me so busy. I will try harder to concentrate on our relationship. I never want you to feel neglected."

"I don't feel neglected. I know you're busy with the team." I wish I could have told him the rumors about him and Tracy, but I didn't want to spoil this fairytale. After dinner I dropped Mike off at his grandmother's. We didn't want the night to end, but he had practice the next morning. I got home and realized he forgot his wallet in my car seat. I would take it to him first thing in the morning.

The next morning, I woke up and drove to Mike's house. When I pulled up I noticed his car was not in the driveway. I saw his grandmother having breakfast in the kitchen window. I rang the doorbell. She welcomed me with a smile. She had beautiful silver hair, and was always beautifully dressed, even early in the morning.

"Patrice, how are you dear? I'm sorry, but Michael had basketball practice this morning."

"Yes, I know. I just came by to bring him his wallet. He forgot it in my car last night."

"Oh, well I will leave it for him in the kitchen, his favorite place. That boy loves to eat. Would you like some breakfast?"

"No, that's fine. I'm going back home my mom is cooking as well. Thanks for asking."

"You're welcome sweetie. How's school going? You're a senior, like Michael, right?" Before I could answer she continued talking. "Patrice, I don't know you well. You have been seeing my grandson for some time now. I don't get too much in Michael's business, but I want to tell you to not to waste time getting too serious in a relationship at your age. There's a whole lot to see in this world. I just wish I heard that when I was your age. I fell in love too fast. I didn't pay attention to the tug in my heart by God. You see, God was trying to take me in a different direction. Instead, I chose my own path. Patrice, what I'm trying to say to you is let God direct your footsteps. With Him on your side, you never have to worry about wasting time."

"Okay, thanks." I didn't know what to say after that lecture. I did think about what she said on my way home. Whatever she was trying to say, she didn't want to come out and say, "Child, my grandson is a dog!" I laughed about her being that blunt. I got lost in thought on my drive home, letting God direct my footsteps.

When I got in the house, there wasn't a soul in sight. There was a note on the refrigerator from my mom saying she went to the mall, her Saturday routine. My brother was probably at a friend's house. I had the whole place to myself. I cooked some breakfast and watch a little TV. I kept thinking about what Mike's grandmother said to me. It was her first time ever talking to me like that, as if she was trying to save me from destruction. The blaring horn in my driveway interrupted my thoughts. It was my mom's boyfriend, Malcolm. He was never my favorite person. He was in and out of my mom's life at his convenience. He's been in my life since I was a little girl. I resented him. He could've had such an influence on me as I grew up, but he didn't take much interest. Sometimes the only word he spoke was *hello*. I always thought that was strange, but was use to the distance.

"Is anybody home? Patrice, are you in there?"

"Yeah. Hey, Malcolm, I'm in the kitchen."

"Is your mother here? We were supposed to go to the movies."

"No, she's not. She left a note that said she was going to the mall."

"Oh, okay. I'll just wait until she gets back. So how are you? Your mom said you were doing well in school."

"Yeah, I'm doing pretty well. I'll be going to look at colleges."

"I remember when you were a little girl. I always knew you would do something with your life. I just want you to know that you can do anything you put your mind to. Don't let anybody tell you different." I didn't hear my mom come in, I was so in tuned to what Malcolm said to me. I wish he talked to me like that growing up. That small piece of advice was priceless. I always knew I could do anything, now it was confirmed.

I didn't leave the house the rest of the afternoon. Kim called and invited me to go bowling with Tiffany, Amber, and Lisa. I wasn't feeling up to bowling.

"No, that's cool, but call me when you get in, and let me know how it was."

"All right chica, I promise. Love you." I never heard Kim say those words to me.

"I love you too." I used that day to clean up my room and reminisce with old pictures. I fell asleep, and was awakened by the phone. I thought my mom or brother would answer it, but no one was home, so I picked up.

"Patrice! Patrice!" It was Kim's mom screaming and crying. "Come to the hospital. It's Kim!" My body went completely numb. She kept screaming, "My baby, Kim!" I didn't waste any time getting to the hospital. I parked in the Emergency parking lot and sprinted into the waiting room, in Intensive Care. All of Kim's family was there along with her friends' parents.

Kim's dad said that she was in a car accident. A car sped out of control on the expressway. Tiffany, Amber, and Lisa suffered a couple of bad bruises. Kim was in critical condition. Her nurse was only allowing one person at a time to visit because of her condition. As I waited for her family to finish visiting, I thought about what I would say. I was really nervous to see her, I didn't know what to expect. Kim's mom walked up to me in tears.

"Patrice, you can go in now." I walked down the long corridor and cried. I didn't want to see my best friend in a hospital bed. I walked in her room and was shocked. She was hooked to what seemed like hundreds of machines. All I could do was rub her hair and stare deep into her eyes. She was fighting for her life, unable to speak, forced to write on a pad. She wrote, *Patrice, don't cry. I'm glad you're here. I love you so much and I'm sorry this happened. I was supposed to call you when I got in the house.* Tears fell like buckets of water on her bed. *Don't cry, I'm going to a better place. You still have a job to do down here. Don't waste time with Mike. You deserve better. Be patient and wait on the Lord. Don't be afraid to let him go. I have cherished this friendship we have shared. Don't ever forget our times together. I'll see you soon.* That was the last thing she wrote, and she closed her eyes. My best friend was gone.

"Kim, don't leave me!"

CHAPTER 4

—◊—

My mom and brother were in the waiting room. Mom was the only one who could calm me down and pick me up from the floor. I sat in the waiting room, and felt so empty. I cried for so long, everything around me was dark. Why did God have to take my best friend? I wished I were in the car with her. I blamed myself for the accident, for declining the invitation to go bowling. Maybe I could've saved her in some way. Why couldn't God have taken me instead?

We left the hospital with Kim's distraught family. Tiffany, Amber, and Lisa were there too, crying. Their bruises made me angry. I blamed them for my friend's death. I didn't want anything to do with them. Everybody was emotionally and physically drained. Kim's mom was talking about funeral arrangements.

Once at home, I went straight to bed and cried myself to sleep. I woke up the next morning, it was pouring down rain. I called Kim to see what her plans were, to brighten this gloomy day. Dialing her number hit me like a ton of bricks, that my best friend was really gone. Sobbing into my pillow, I heard voices downstairs.

"Patrice, are you up? You have company." My mom was outside of my bedroom. The only person it could be was Mike. And he was the last person I wanted to see.

"Okay," I said between sobs. "I'll be there in a minute." I tried my best to not look like a zombie, a cozy sweatshirt and sweat pants. I threw my hair in a ponytail. That was as good as it was going to get. My mom was cooking eggs, bacon, and grits. Mike didn't waste any time eating everything in sight. I just stood there in the kitchen. He grabbed me, and held me tight.

"Patrice," he said. "I'm so sorry. Do you need anything?"

"No, I'm fine." My words slurred and didn't even make

sense. I didn't want to sit and chat. The pain was so severe it could have made me faint.

"Have some breakfast," said Mom. "You haven't eaten anything since yesterday."

"Mom, I'm fine. I really don't have an appetite yet."

"Well, have some juice at least."

Mike and I both sat there in silence. I had nothing to say. I guess he didn't want to say the wrong thing. And all I wanted was to be alone, for this nightmare to end.

"Kim's mom called and said the funeral will be next Saturday." My mom said this as if I wanted to have this conversation. "There will be a lot of family coming from out of town. She asked if you wanted to speak at the funeral."

I wanted to say something, but nothing would come out. I was completely paralyzed. I just got up, went upstairs into my room, and left Mike in the kitchen with my mom.

My alarm buzzed in my ear at 9 a.m. Even though I didn't have the energy, I decided to go to church. My brother was in the bathroom blaring his music. I wasn't really in the dress up mood. I decided to put on blue jeans and my favorite cashmere sweater. I was raised to dress up for church, just not today. When my brother got out of the shower, he peaked in my room.

"Hey, Patrice, are you going to church with me and mom?"

"Yeah."

"Cool. "I really think you need that. It would be good for you. I'll see you downstairs."

When I got downstairs my mom and brother were both waiting for me, sitting down talking and laughing about old memories. The laughter in the house did help ease the pain.

Church was packed. As we were ushered to our seats, the pastor was talking about Kim's life. There was a slide show of her, soft music in the background. I sobbed. I wished I stayed home.

"Kim's life was short on this earth, but she touched many." The congregation nodded to the pastor's words.

"She was a gift from God. And God called her home. I know many of your hearts are sad, ask God to touch those areas where you're weak. Continue to remember the good times you have shared. You all still have a job to complete on the earth." I couldn't believe he said that. *We have a job to complete.* Those were the exact words Kim wrote to me before she died.

The soloist had everyone on their feet. People were screaming out *Jesus* and going around hugging each other. A few people from school came to hug me. Everyone knew how close Kim and I were. I wanted to hold onto every hug and never let go. They were hugging the pain away.

The next day at school, teachers were telling students to talk to the guidance counselor if they were feeling depressed. I didn't plan on pouring out my feelings to a complete stranger. What could she tell me that I didn't already know? At lunch, I sat at the table Kim and I used to share. I was alone. I was shocked by all the love that came from students. I received so many cards. Complete strangers just hugged me. Mike walked in the cafeteria and sat at my table. Tracy stared a hole through me.

"What are you doing here? Aren't you supposed to be in class?"

"Yeah, but I wanted to stop by and check up on you. I know this is hard."

"I'm fine. I just want this day to be over."

"It'll be over soon." He kissed me on my forehead, which was sweet. Tracy got up and left.

"I have basketball practice after school. I was thinking I would come over afterward and spend some time with you. Is that cool?"

"Okay."

After lunch, I sat in Algebra class. I had no idea what the teacher was talking about. I should've been paying attention because Algebra is not my favorite subject. To make matters worse, I had an exam on Friday. The bell rang. I was the first one out to the parking lot.

Tracy was waiting for the school bus. She gave me the meanest look. I was definitely going to have to deal with her sooner or later. I went straight to the mall before going home. I needed to take my mind off things. If I had a job, I would be able to buy more things, but my mom wanted me to focus on school. I bought a few shirts and sweaters. There were a few people from school in the food court. I ate at McDonalds, cold fries and hard nuggets, then went home. Mike was already there waiting for me on the porch.

"Hey, I've been waiting here for about an hour. Didn't you see my missed calls? Is everything ok?"

"Yeah, I was at the mall. I forgot you were stopping by. I'm sorry."

"It's cool as long as you're okay. I can't stay too long, I have a game tomorrow. If you were here sooner, we could've got something to eat."

"That's fine. I just ate. Thanks for stopping by."

"Whoa....Did I do something. I sense a little attitude."

"Yeah, my friend just died!" I snapped.

"Patrice, I don't mean to be insensitive, but it seems like something else is bothering you."

"You know what else is bothering me!"

"What?"

"Tracy, that's what!" I left him standing there on the porch and slammed the door in his face.

My phone rang about ten times before I turned it off. It was Mike calling me. I was tired of wondering what was going on with him. I couldn't forget when Kim said to be patient and wait on the Lord; and that I deserved better. It helped to tell myself every day that I deserve better. Instead of watching TV, I studied for my math test. I had to get at least a B since midterms were coming up. Thank God for multiple choice. Studying must've put me to sleep, when I woke up it was after 11 p.m. I took the pastor's advice from church and prayed. I asked God to give me peace, to take the pain away, and to order my footsteps (advice that was given to me from Mike's grandmother). After that, I didn't know what else to say. I went to bed and slept peacefully for the first time in months.

CHAPTER 5

I was nervous about the math test. My palms were sweaty all day. I was the first one to finish the test. The other students were jealous as I handed my test to Mr. Smith. Studying the night before must have helped after all.

The time between classes made me think of Kim. Her funeral was the next day. It left me sick to my stomach. There was no one to hang out with in the halls, and of course Mike was not one of my favorite people, so I avoided him. Tracy walked towards me on the way to my next class. All of her girlfriends watched as if they knew what she was going to do. She bumped into me with her shoulder. I turned around without thinking. I had a fistful of hair in my hand, threw her to the floor, banged her head against the locker and stomped her with all the strength I had. Every time she tried to get up I would kick her back down.

"Patrice, Patrice, stop!" The sound of Mike's voice broke me out of my trance. Tracy's girlfriends all ran to help her off the floor, her hair all over her head. There was blood on her shirt. I could've killed the girl. Mike walked with me and a teacher to the principal's office. I didn't care about suspension. I was tired of these girls. In the Principal's Office, Tracy and I sat across from each other. The room was silent. Mrs. Washington entered and sat behind her desk.

"You girls should be ashamed of yourselves. You both are seniors and acting like little girls. And you, Miss. Patrice. I understand you're hurting over your friend's death, but this is no way to behave. Tracy, go to the nurse's office and come see me afterward." I feared what Mrs. Washington would say next. "Patrice, I must admit I was wondering when you were going to lose it. I've watched these girls harass you for two years. I admire the way you usually handle yourself. What finally set you off?"

"She bumped me on purpose, and I just lost it."

"I knew it had to be something she did. You remind me of myself when I was in school. Girls gave me a hard time, too. I'm sure Tracy won't do that again. I'm going to have to suspend both of you for one day. Both of you need to be here to prepare for your exams." Mrs. Washington called after me before I even set a foot in the hallway. "Patrice, if this had anything to do with a boy, it's not worth it. You have your whole life ahead of you. You are a beautiful girl and believe that you deserve better. Trust God has something more. If you ever need to talk, you know where to find me."

"Okay." I was surprised that Mrs. Washington even cared. She was definitely someone I could open up to about my feelings on Kim's death. I was relieved to only get a one day suspension. I couldn't afford to miss school. My brother waited for me at my car. He must've been there a long time. Everyone else was gone.

"Yo, Patrice, I heard you beat Tracy up! I heard she had blood all over. I wish I was there. Don't nobody mess up with my sister. I would've had your back."

"Yeah, way back." We both burst into laughter.

My mom was home cooking dinner. I still loved the smell of her home cooked meals. Desmond couldn't wait to tell her about my fight.

"Patrice, whipped this girl in school today. The girl was bleeding and everything."

"What! Patrice what happened?!"

"This girl bumped me on purpose in school today. She's been testing me for two years. It was just a matter of time before she felt my wrath." Desmond and I bust out laughing.

"Patrice, I'm glad to see you laughing again, but this is not funny. Were you suspended?"

"Yes, but only for one day. Mrs. Washington was cool about the whole thing. She even shared how she had problems with girls in high school."

"Well, I'm glad you only got suspended for one day. And I'm glad that girl got what she deserves. Nobody messes with my baby." We all laughed. "Now both of you set the table, dinner is ready.

CHAPTER 6

———ww———

I dreaded the day of Kim's funeral. The image of her in a casket hurt. I wore a black skirt and white blouse with black stilettos. I pulled my hair back into a bun and wore my black Chanel sunglasses. I had to be at Kim's family's house first thing in the morning since I was riding with Kim's family in the limo. When I arrived, there were people standing outside. A lot of kids came from school to show support. Walking through the crowd of people in the house made it difficult to find Kim's mom. The last place I looked was Kim's room. She was sitting on her bed holding a cheerleading jacket.

"My baby is gone." Tears smeared her makeup and soaked the jacket. Kim's mom was a beautiful woman with high cheekbones, almond-shaped eyes, and long wavy hair. I sat next to her, and held her in my arms until she mustered the strength to join the guests downstairs.

We walked to the limo after the pastor prayed. I was honored that Kim's mom asked me to join the family to the church. We all sat, and cried to ourselves. Once I stepped foot into the church, everything blurred, but I could still see the hundreds of people that came out. People were in the balcony standing against the wall. Not an empty seat was left for Kim. I sat in the second row facing the casket, white with silver trim. She looked beautiful. Her hair was perfectly combed. It fell passed her shoulders with little curls at the ends. She was wearing a cream suit with brown stilettos. Her nails were nicely groomed, and her makeup was flawless. She looked liked a china doll, so peaceful. I must've been standing at the casket too long. One of the ushers had to escort me back to my seat. The choir sang *I'll Fly Away*. Mike walked in and sat next to my mom. He was wearing a black suit with dark sunglasses. I had not talked to him since the fight, but was glad to see him.

"Kim's work here is done. But you still have a job to do. Don't let the devil steal your life away. Ask God what he intends for you to do. He has a plan for you. Those of you who haven't accepted Christ: it's not too late. He's waiting for you with open arms."

After the service, I volunteered to be a flower girl. That was the least I could do for my friend, since I didn't speak. Mike tried to get my attention but I kept looking straight ahead. I wasn't ready to speak to him just yet. The cemetery was my last good-bye to Kim. As her body was lowered six feet under, I screamed out one last time.

"Kiiiiiiim!"

—◊◊◊—

I stayed home the next day from church. I couldn't bear seeing those same faces from the funeral. I definitely needed time to heal. I thought about giving Mrs. Washington a visit in school the next day, if it wasn't for my suspension, that is. Since I had not talked to my dad in awhile, I called him and suggested I come down to Florida to visit next weekend. He answered on the first ring.

"Hey, baby girl, I was just thinking about you. I am deeply sorry about your friend. If you need to get away for a few days let me know."

"I'm doing fine, and that's why I was calling. I would like to come there to visit soon. I was thinking about coming to visit you for a few days."

"Sure, just give me the dates, and your ticket will be waiting for you at the airport. You know how we do."

"How about next weekend?"

"You got it, I will call you once I make the reservations. Listen, I hate to run so soon, but I'm at a building site. Give my love to your mom and Desmond. I'll call you later tonight. Be strong. I love you."

"I love you too." It felt good that I would be getting a way for a few days. I was excited to spend some quality time with my dad. Mom was excited for me getting away for a few days. My parents had always maintained a close friendship, despite the divorce.

Sometimes I wished they would get back together so we could be a family again.

My dad lived right next to South Beach. He bragged about the beautiful weather and trendy restaurants. Since it was bound to be warm everyday, I decided to pack my favorite jeans, tank tops, flip flops and, of course, bathing suits. I planned on spending a lot of time at the beach.

I was a zombie upon returning to school. Alone, without Kim or Mike. I wish I could have gone straight to college. I'm glad that I didn't have to deal with Tracy. She was suspended for a week for instigating the fight. It was all for the best. I was glad; I couldn't take seeing her in the hallways.

Lunchtime was my least favorite. I hated eating the slop they fed us, and looking for people to sit with. No one wants to be a lonely loser. Someone screamed my name across the cafeteria.

"Patrice! Over here!" I'd been avoiding the girls since the accident, but had to face them eventually. They were all still shaken up. We all were.

"We all feel terrible about what happened," said Lisa. "The drunk driver came out of nowhere running a red light. Before we knew it we were slammed up against a tree." She began to cry. This was the first time I heard what happened. I avoided listening to all the details. I just wanted my friend back.

"I know it wasn't your fault," I said. "Kim is in a peaceful place now."

"Anytime you want to hang out and get your mind off things," said Tiffany. "Give us a call. You don't have to be a stranger."

"Thanks."

"So do you have anything planned for the Christmas break, there are a few parties we're going to crash." Tiffany was always the party animal of the bunch. We didn't have anything in common.

"I'm going to see my dad in Miami this weekend, but my schedule is open after Miami."

"Well don't forget to soak up the sun for us. I wish I was

going. What a great vacation, I'm so jealous. When you get back we have to hit the malls and get manicures and pedicures, it'll be a girls' day out."

"Now you're talking. I never turn down a shopping spree."

We all burst out in laughter. I knew Kim would be proud that we were still enjoying our lives just like she would have.

CHAPTER 7

—w—

The airport was packed. Everyone was in a hurry. I wondered where each person was traveling to. I always found the airport so fascinating. After checking my luggage and going through security, I felt like I was hit by a truck. I found my gate, and collapsed into the closest seat.

"Hello, young lady now where might you be traveling to?" I was surprised that this little old lady wanted to know where I was going. She had a Caribbean accent.

"I'm going to Florida to visit my dad."

"Ahhh...Florida. What a wonderful place to visit. My husband and I would travel there all the time."

"Do you still travel together?"

"No, my Frankie died years ago. He's now with the Lord. But that doesn't stop me from wanting to see the world. God created it, and I still have lots to see. I'm off to Italy to visit a girlfriend."

"Wow! Italy. That sounds like so much fun."

"Fun indeed. You may be young, but always think big because we serve a big God. He has so many things he wants you to see. It's a big world out there. He's just waiting for you to jump in."

The loud speaker muffled instructions. "Passengers flying to Florence, Italy please have your boarding passes ready. We are starting to board."

"Well, that's me. Enjoy your time to with your dad and don't forget to dream Big dreams." And just like that she was gone.

Dad was waiting for me at baggage claim. He picked me up, and spun me around. He's been doing that since I was a kid. It still makes me laugh.

"Tricie Pooh, a.k.a. Mike Tyson."

"I swear, nothing gets by in this family."

"Yeah, Des told me about your little brawl. Did you use the moves I taught you?"

"Yeah, dad, whatever." I grabbed my suitcase, and we hit the road. Dad always kept a nice car. This time it was a black on black Mercedes Benz coupe hard top convertible.

"So, Patrice are you dating anybody?" I hated these father daughter conversations. They always made me feel so uncomfortable.

"Kind of. There is this guy, Mike, at school. He's a basketball player, but lately we've been having some problems."

"What kind of problems? Do I have to come up there?"

"No, dad, it's not like that. It's just that I've been hearing about him talking to some girl."

"Hmmmm....my advice: he's not worth talking to my princess. You deserve so much more. I mean that. You're a diamond. If it's not making you happy, walk away. Life is too short." Those simple words meant a lot coming from my dad. Now only if I can find it in myself to believe.

The drive way was long and winding with a three-car garage. My dad's house was a museum. He said he was having his home built, but I didn't picture it like this. There were marble countertops in the kitchen, a spiral staircase, and a huge foyer area. He even had a movie theatre.

"Daddy, you're really doing it big since the last time I visited."

"I told you I was moving on up like the Jeffersons." He brought me to my room. There was a flat screen TV, king size bed, and I even had my own bathroom.

"Make yourself at home. We have a long day tomorrow. I want to take you around to visit some people. The beach is right across the street. Feel free to soak up some sun before we leave tomorrow afternoon. I love you."

"Love you too, daddy."

I woke up the next morning and forgot where I was. A big smile came across my face. I jumped up, and wanted to get to the beach as soon as possible. I showered; and threw on a pair of jean shorts and white tank top over my bathing suit. I grabbed some sun tan lotion, sunglasses, a beach towel, bottled water, and fruit. That was enough, I was on my way to the beach.

Everyone looked like supermodels. All of the girls had glowing tans, and the guys looked like they came off the runway. You definitely have to be in shape to live in this town. The beach wasn't too crowded and I was able to buy a beach chair. I plopped down in the perfect spot, and stared in awe at the big waves, music to my ears. As I laid on my back with my eyes closed for what seemed like hours, I was startled by a voice.

"Is this spot taken?" He was beautiful; tall, complexion dipped in bronze, perfect straight teeth, high cheekbones, and abs cut just right.

"No, it's not taken." I couldn't believe that's all I said. I couldn't even think of my name.

"My name is Sanai and yours?"

"Uhhhh, my name is Patrice."

"So, do you come here often Patrice?"

"No, I'm actually here just here visiting my dad for the weekend. How about you?"

"I live here. I'm from Hawaii, but been living here doing the model thing."

"Oh, you're a model?"

"What is that supposed to mean?"

"I don't know."

"Don't tell me you believe the stereotypes. Stuck up, bunch of different girls, party animal." I couldn't help but laugh.

"To tell you the truth, it's not like that at all. I'm quite the opposite of that. I'm a homebody. I date one girl at a time, and don't think I'm all that handsome. So tell me about yourself."

"Well...I'm a senior in high school and plan to go to college in the fall majoring in Broadcast Journalism."

"That's cool. Our dreams are truly up to us. No one else can make them happen but us. I will eventually like to go to law school, that's why I'm modeling, to help cover the cost. Well, I'll let you soak up this sun I have a few friends waiting for me. You are beautiful by the way, not just your outer beauty, but a beautiful spirit. Don't stop smiling. It was nice to meet you."

"It was nice to meet you too." Once he walked off, I put my sunglasses on, plugged in my iPod, and got some much needed relaxation.

Dad's car was in the driveway. I was starving. His fiancé, Nicole, was in the kitchen. I talked to her a few times on the phone. She seemed nice, and my dad seemed to be in love.

"Hi, Patrice," she said. "You're even prettier in person."

"Thanks, Nicole. So when is the big wedding day?"

"Well, your dad and I decided to have it next summer so more friends and family can attend. It will be right here in Miami. When I go dress shopping I would like you to come and help an old lady out."

"I would love to. I'm so happy for you."

"Thank you, sweetie." Nicole was a beautiful woman with dark brown skin and hazel green eyes. Her hair was jet black, and flowed down her back. She had no children, and dated my dad for five years.

"Your dad is in the den watching a movie."

"Daddy!"

"Down here, Patrice. Nicole and I are taking you to this great restaurant tonight."

"Great! Because I'm starving"

"So what do you think about my future wife?"

"I think she's beautiful. We always had good phone conversations. Very nice."

"She is. She has been here for me through the ups and downs. I never thought I would marry again, but never say never. Start getting ready; this restaurant fills up pretty quick."

"You don't have to tell me twice, I love to eat."

We went to an upscale restaurant. Once we all hopped out of Dad's Range Rover, the valet rushed over to park it. Dad handed him cash and patted him on the shoulder. He always taught me that if you pay a little extra, people will try harder to take care of your possessions. I was in awe of the restaurant. It was very dim, engulfed in beautiful tones. The hostess gave us the choice to sit outside, or inside, next to the streaming waterfall. We stayed in, away from all of the nightlife. It was nice to get to know Nicole a little better. She was like a friend inviting me to go shopping. She really understood me.

"So, how do you like it back home?"

"It's fine. I can't wait to graduate from High School. All of the cattiness is driving me crazy."

"I definitely know what you're talking about. Been there, done that."

"What did you do to get passed it?"

"I chose to love myself and ignore them. If you do that, you win." I thought deeply about what she said about loving myself, but it was hard for me to understand. How do I just love myself? I hear it all of the time, but it's just not an easy thing for me to do. Nicole and I talked for the rest of the night.

I woke up with an excruciating headache. It must have been from all of the laughing at dinner. We didn't get in until midnight. I was dreading the return back to reality, back to school, back to having to face Mike; it made me cringe. So this was the last day in Miami, and I was going to make it a memorable one. Daddy was down stairs cooking a feast. I could smell the bacon through the walls.

"What's up, baby girl? Today is our day. I want to take you to my favorite place."

"Great! But before we go anywhere I need to eat. That place was fancy last night, but the portions were for a five year old.

"Girl, you are crazy."

We both laughed over pancakes, eggs, bacon, and home fries. I didn't think I could do the whole Dad and daughter day. What I wanted was a bed and a remote. But after a shower and getting dressed, I got a burst of energy, and peace since Kim's death. I didn't know where dad was taking me. I wore something comfortable.

"Patrice, you ready to go!" Dad was carrying his camera.

"What's the camera for?"

"Us. Let's go."

We cruised Miami with the top down, wind blowing through my hair, the sound of the ocean. I never felt so peaceful in my whole life. This trip was worth it. The road steeped. We reached the top of the mountain that overlooked Miami.

"I have never seen anything so beautiful in my whole life."

"We're here. This is my favorite place. I like to come here and reflect on my life, talk to God and just get away from the fast life."

"I wanted to bring you here because I wanted to tell you as your father, in my most favorite place, that you're beautiful inside and out. Don't let anyone tell you anything different. You have grown into a woman. This is a very important time in your life. Every decision you make can impact your destiny. The decisions that I made as a boy are still affecting me today as a man. I guess what I'm trying to say is, develop a closer relationship with the Lord Jesus Christ. He will show you who you are, sweet heart. You won't have to guess. He has your blue print for your whole life. You may not understand this at your age, but I want to share with you what my parents shared with me. I want you to know that you can have a life that is not dependent on having a boyfriend just so you can feel popular or important. You can have a relationship with Jesus Christ, who is there to make you whole. He will fill any insecurity you have with His love. It's ok when you meet a guy and simply tell him "It was nice to meet you." Not everyone deserves your phone number. It's not healthy to cling to a man just because he thinks you're attractive. The truth, baby girl, is that there are going to be a lot of young men as you get older that are going to find you attractive, but it doesn't mean they are the one that God has for you. You want who God has. Not a counterfeit. Maybe that's why you're here, so you can get fatherly wisdom, or whatever I have to say, if that counts as wisdom. But listen. Any boy that doesn't treat you like royalty is the counterfeit."

The sun set below the horizon as the ocean's waves beat against the rocks at the base of the mountain. My dad wiped my tears and smoothed my hair away from my face. He held me close and kissed my forehead. I never wanted to let him go. He whispered I love you. The night was perfect.

The next morning came like a shooting bullet. I groaned, Dad scheduled an early flight. He didn't know I only see 6 a.m. on week days.

"Patrice, are you up? Today is the big day."

"Ughhhh!" The shower had me deep in thought. My dad was right about Mike. Was he really just a counterfeit? How could he say he's not the one and never even meet him? The airport wasn't as crowded as back home, especially since normal people are sleeping at the crack of dawn. Dad walked me up to the check out desk. We held each other tight.

"I have to get to work. Call me as soon as you land. I love you."

"I love you, too." I took my boarding pass and was on my way. There was a familiar voice behind me.

"So you were going to leave without saying goodbye. That's not nice." It was Sanai. How did he know what time my flight was leaving? Why didn't he tell me that he would be at the airport? Where was he traveling to?

"Sanai! Where are you going?"

"I actually have a fashion show in New York this week."

"That's great!"

"How about we go get something to eat before our flights comes."

"Sure, I'm starving. Let's crash McDonald's." We ate pancakes and sausage, and talked about his modeling career. He visited his family in Hawaii only on holidays. He asked me about my family, and goals after high school. I told him my interest on going to NYU, to someday be on TV reporting the news.

"I can't wait to get out of high school."

"Well if you can learn anything from me, don't rush high school, even though you may hate it. You will never get these years back. Trust me. I know. I used to say the same thing when I was in high school. Now I look back, and wish that I would've appreciated those times in my life. I wanted so fast to grow up. Now it's all about bills, bills, bills." I really didn't want to leave Sanai, I knew we would never see each other again.

"I'm sorry, but I have to go."

"Give me a great big hug." He towered over me holding my head to his chest. "I had a great time with you Patrice, and I hope that I will see you again."

"I had a great time with you too. It was so nice to meet you." I walked to security and never looked back.

CHAPTER 8

—⁓—

I missed my dad. All those words of wisdom shaped my self esteem, but the outcome of those conversations only last for about a week. Sometimes I wonder what my life would have been like if my mom and dad stayed together; just the thought of it brings tears to my eyes. Moving to Miami to be with my Dad made me laugh, he would really be in my business, but at least there, it felt like home, sometimes more so than my actual one.

The plane reached over a pile of fluffy clouds. I felt closer to God; it was a feeling of peace. It was as if He was speaking to me: *everything is going to be all right.* I closed my eyes and fell asleep.

We landed in Atlanta. I woke up to the pilot's voice. The flight attendant told me to put my seat up. I wanted to ask her why she didn't wake me up when drinks were served. They seem to bother you about everything else. The lady next to me all of sudden wanted to have a conversation about my life. I don't mind talking to people, but gosh, couldn't she see I just woke up! I answered her with yes or no until she understood I'd rather be left alone. When it was our turn to get off the plane I grabbed my bag and sprinted to baggage claim where mom was waiting for me.

"Hey, baby girl, how was your trip?!" I ran into my mom's arms where it felt safe. I couldn't wait to tell her about dad's fiancé and Sanai, but first, I needed food. Mom went to get the car while I gathered my things. There was someone else in the car. Malcolm. I could've sworn she told me that they were through. I opened the car door and tried to force a smile.

"Hey, Malcolm!"

"Hey, Patrice, how was your trip?"

"Fine." I couldn't believe mom invited Malcolm. I was looking forward to sharing my trip with her, but now it was ruined by Mr. Man. All I could do without screaming was shut my eyes and force myself to sleep. Maybe when I opened my eyes he would be gone.

I woke up in the driveway. Thank God we were home. I didn't have to listen to the oldies-but-goodies station. Desmond ran out of the house when he saw the car. He almost knocked me down with a bear hug.

"Gosh, Desmond, don't try to kill me! I missed you too."

"Whatever, Patrice, I'm going to miss reading your diary."

"Mom!"

"Patrice, don't you pay that boy any mind. Now get upstairs, unpack, get ready for supper, and no, Desmond, don't even think about going anywhere tonight with those grades, you need to be going out in those books." Mom always did have a sense of humor.

My room was exactly how I left it. Mom could've at least straightened up. I really did need to work on my sloppiness. Lesson learned, mom. I knew I had to end things with Michael. Dad's advice made a lot of sense. If someone cheats on you, then they're really not for you. After I unpacked and laid on the bed, I couldn't help but to start thinking about Michael and how I would end things. It didn't make any sense for me to put myself through any more drama, and I didn't want to return to school to anymore fights. I would let go and focus on school.

"Patrice, dinner is ready!"

"Where's Malcolm?" I tried to sound surprised.

"Oh, he had to go to work."

"I thought you weren't going to see him anymore."

"Patrice, now don't be up in my business. Sometimes grown folks go through things. We're O.K. now." I hated the fact that she still talked me to like I was a child. He wasn't right for her. She was getting upset so I didn't ask any more questions.

"Daddy, is doing great in Miami."

"Well, your father always knew how to pick them."

"I also met a guy on the beach, his name is Sanai. He's

soooo cute. And he is from Hawaii. I'm really glad I went. It was exactly what I needed."

"I'm really glad that you enjoyed yourself, Patrice. You and your father should spend more time with each other. And since he's doing so great, he shouldn't have any problems flying you out there more often. So, do you have a picture of this Sanai?"

"No, only in my head."

"Okay. What about Mike?"

"I've decided to end things with him. I can't trust anything he says anymore."

"Well, I'm sure glad that you came to your senses about that boy. I knew he was bad news from the moment I met him." Now I really knew how she felt about him. All of this time she was just being nice to him because of me. "Patrice, at this time in your life you really need to focus on school, the boys will always be there. Set some goals and start applying to college. I will schedule some visits to colleges on your goal list. At least that will get your mind off of Mike, and start focusing on what's important." Mom was right. The only thing that was important was getting good grades so that I would be accepted into college. Ending things with Mike would be hard.

I got up an hour early to choose the coolest outfit. Black leggings and long purple v-neck sweater. My black riding boots completed the outfit together perfectly. I wore my hair straight, and put a little bit of purple eye shadow on and eyeliner. All I needed was my watermelon lip gloss and I was ready.

"Patrice, I didn't know the club was open this early in the morning."

"Shut up, Desmond, you just mad that you can't look this good."

"Leave your sister alone." Mom butting in again.

"Patrice, I'm going to need you to pick Desmond up from basketball practice this evening. I'm working late tonight. Have a nice day at school, and Patrice, remember our talk last night. Love you."

"Talk," Desmond had to always know what was going on.

"What talk?"

"Mind your business, big head. Get in the car."

Everyone's eyes fell on me in homeroom. The fight with Tracy was still fresh in their minds. I left the past in the past. My homeroom teacher walked over to me.

"Patrice, Mrs. Washington would like to see you."

I was excited to see Mrs. Washington, but a little nervous why she wanted to see me on my first day back. I walked into her office, she was on the phone.

"Okay, sweetie, have a fantastic day today, see you later." She was giggling like a two year old. A part of me didn't want to see this side of Mrs. Washington, but it was nice to see that human side of her.

"Patrice, good to see you. Close the door and have a seat." The chair was comfortable, and the lights made me sleepy. There was an odor of Lysol and rubbing alcohol. For some reason it made my stomach growl. Lunch was so far away. "So, how does it feel to be back in school?"

"I feel great. I just want to focus on my school work and start applying to colleges. I've been putting that off a lot lately."

"That's great to hear, and if you need any help writing your college essay, please don't hesitate to ask. I would love to help. I'm actually glad that you're preparing for college, it's the reason I wanted to see you. I have a friend whose a professor at New York University and I told her all about you. NYU is such a great school. If you would like me to set up a visit, let me know. Talk to your mother about it and let me know what you decide."

"Thanks, Mrs. Washington. Kim and I dreamed about going to NYU together. I would love to visit. Thank you so much!"

"You're quite welcome, Patrice. I believe in you. You can go far. Just continue to stay focused. Welcome back." I walked out of the office so excited, and happy that Mrs. Washington was willing to help me get in to my dream school. She's someone to aspire to be like.

I raised my hand and asked questions in my algebra class, and even asked for help after school. This time I was serious, I had to boost my GPA and start thinking about college, specifically NYU, since this was my senior year. I was looking forward to my next class, TV News Reporting. I was glad that this was a part of the curriculum, since it would be my major in college. I had the opportunity to learn how to write news stories, not hard news, but what was going on in our school in terms of sports and the next school dance. I scheduled random interviews with students in the hallway about the Christmas holiday. One of the students asked on camera about my fight and screamed *beat down*. It was hilarious, but my teacher refused to air it, fearing the start of another altercation. Our final project was due in May, and I refused to get less than an A.

Mike was standing right in front of me looking more handsome than he ever did. "Hey, Patrice, there you are. I've been looking all over for you." I couldn't believe this was my first time seeing him since I left for Miami. This was as good a time as any to break the news.

"Hey, stranger. I decided to meet with my Algebra teacher, I have a test on Friday."

"Well, looks like somebody is getting serious about college."

"Yes, I am," I smiled.

"Well, I don't want to keep you from your work, but I would like to talk to you later when you have some time. I'm about to go to practice, I'll call you later."

"Okay." That's all I could say. So much for breaking up with him. For some reason I was more nervous than usual. I was glad that it ended that way because I wasn't ready to tell him that I no longer wanted to see him. *Lord, please give me the strength.*

I was completely drained when I got home. My algebra teacher really broke a lot of the problems down that I didn't understand; why did it have to be so difficult? I was surprised my mom wasn't home, usually there would be the smell of food cooking, or the TV blaring in the living room. When I went to the kitchen there was a note on the fridge:

Went out for dinner, tried to wait for you and tried calling you numerous times. Left overs are in the fridge. Be home soon.
Love, Mom.

I was glad not to have dinner with them. The last thing I wanted was to listen to Malcolm's corny jokes, and my mom cracking up and wondering why I wasn't joining in on the corniness. I opened the fridge and took out the left over spaghetti, Mike's favorite, and popped it in the microwave. I walked into my room to some mail on my bed. It was a letter from my dad. I tore through the envelope. In red letters it read: *Remember what I told you. You, my darling, deserve to be treated like the queen you are. Never accept nothing but God's best. You already know what to do.* A tear dropped down my cheek, I felt like my dad was next to me, coaching me to take that next step. I wish I could have disappeared and forget about what was going on in my teenage drama. I felt myself drifting further and further from the truth. I had to tell Mike that we could no longer be together. The sooner I did that, the sooner I could move on, but for now all I wanted was to go to sleep, and that was the truth.

Thank God for school half-days. I didn't care why, and I wasn't going to ask any questions. Maybe they made a mistake. I wanted to go shopping for some gifts for Christmas. Tiffany invited me to a party. I was excited to go. One of the star basketball players was having a party at his house, or should I say mansion. Both of his parents were top neurosurgeons and had big bucks. I had no idea what I was going to wear. As soon as I got into school I ran right into Tiffany.

"Hey, Patrice!" She was so bubbly, even at 8 a.m.

"What's Up?"

"Me and the girls were going to crash the mall. Would you like to come?"

"Sure. That's where I was going anyway. I'll meet you after school." Tiffany was one of those girls that had everything. She was always very nice and Kim liked her a lot. A lot of the girls were jealous of her, but it never seemed to faze her. I was happy that we would be hanging out and getting to know each other. I pulled my last book out of my locker and had seen Tracy talking to Mike. I felt a huge knot form in my throat and travel to my stomach. I used all of my strength not to vomit all over the floor, to not draw attention to myself, or run off in a jealous rage. I quietly closed my locker and walked to my last class.

I had no idea what my Chemistry teacher was talking about. All I heard was "blah, blah, blah, blah." I could hardly breathe in anticipation for the bell to ring. I was the first one out when it finally chimed, and Tiffany and the rest of the girls were waiting for me out front. I couldn't wait to hit the mall with my new crew. We all piled in Tiffany's Range Rover, she opened up the sunroof and blasted Usher, and with that we headed for the mall.

"So, Patrice, how was your trip?" Lisa asked over the wind blowing in my ear, and the music blaring in my other ear.

"It was great! The weather was awesome everyday, and I met a really cute guy."

"Do Tell!" Tiffany screamed over all of the noise.

"Well, his name is Sanai, and he's a model from Hawaii."

"Well, the next time you go, you have to take us with you. It could be our first girls trip. Hey, maybe we can plan something for senior week, that would be so much fun." Tiffany screamed louder than before.

"Cool!" Just the thought of that made me very excited. I never had a girls trip before.

"We should start planning it soon unless you want to crash at my dad's. I'm sure he wouldn't mind."

"Well, then it's a plan," Amber chimed in. A plan it was.

Everyone in school ended up at the mall. I saw a few people from my Algebra class asking if I had studied and wanted to get together. All of a sudden I became Miss Popular in the classroom. I guess they all noticed that I was about my business this year and I practically knew all of the answers during our practice quiz. I agreed to a group study session in the library and felt good about helping my classmates. As we walked in and out of the stores, there wasn't a lot that caught my attention. I wanted to get something to wear to the party. I had an image in my head, but wasn't seeing it in front of my eyes. I promised myself I wouldn't buy anything unless I absolutely loved it. Tiffany spotted a pair of Charles David tie up stilettos. I must admit, they were hot. They had to cost a pretty penny, but wouldn't dare ask how much. My mother always taught me that it was tacky to ask someone how much something cost.

I watched Tiffany pull out the plastic and off we went. We went to Abercrombie and Fitch. Amber bought a pair of jeans with a purple t-shirt that read *Dollface*. Lisa and I were the only ones who didn't buy anything. As we walked towards Bloomingdales, I heard angles sing. I spotted the perfect fuchsia dress. It was long sleeved and above the knee, but not too short, with a gold zipper zipped up the back. It was fire. All I needed was a pair of fishnet stockings and knee high boots. It was the perfect outfit for the party. I was also missing money. The dress was nearly $100. I didn't want to tease myself in trying it on, and my mom would kill me after locking me up until I was thirty if I put it on her credit card. I walked passed the dress without turning back, but heard it silently calling me, *Patrice, Patrice...wear me...wear me.* I ignored the calls and forced myself out of Bloomingdales before I did something regretful.

We were hungry, so we crashed the food court and ordered Chinese. They had the best lo mein noodles and egg rolls. Finding a table was almost impossible, but we spotted one in the corner a way from all of the chaos. We all laughed how we all had so much in common, and planned to hang out more often.

"So, Patrice, are you still talking to Mike," Tiffany asked. Mike had been the furthest thing from my mind since I was back from Miami, and I hadn't yet talked to him about my feelings. After seeing him talking to Tracy he was more of a distant memory.

"No, we're not as close as we use to be."

"Oh, I'm sorry. I didn't mean to bring up sad feelings."

"No, that's okay. It's just that we haven't had closure yet."

"Isn't he with Tracy now?" Amber asked like that was old news.

"I'm not sure what he's doing. I've just been trying to focus on my school work." Just then, Mike and Tracy walked by the food court hand in hand. It was as if everything around us stopped. Was I dreaming? The answer to Amber's question was walking right passed us.

CHAPTER 9

The ride back home to the school parking lot was very quiet. No one wanted to say anything to hurt my feelings; the girls knew I was still in shock. My mind kept racing about what Mike had to talk to me about. Did he want to tell me that his relationship with Tracy was real, that he no longer wanted to be with me anymore? Even though my plan was to break it off with him, I wasn't prepared for the rejection.

We parked in the lot and I snapped out of my nightmare. The girls all hopped out of the car and gave me a big hug, as if to say everything is going to be okay. Before I got into my car, Tiffany yelled out.

"Patrice, don't forget about the party. It's going to be so much fun! Call me if you need to talk."

I forgot all about the party, but felt a tinge of excitement when she mentioned it.

"I won't," I said, trying to force back tears. "I'll see you in school tomorrow." With that, my new best friends drove off, and I stood there thinking about Mike, who was a friend that I now lost. My phone rang nonstop on the way home. The only person it could be was my mom, since I didn't tell her my plans after school. I decided to wait until I got home before I told her my devastating news.

My mom was pulling groceries out of the car. I immediately burst into tears, jumped out of my car, and ran to her and collapsed into her arms.

"Patrice, Patrice, what's wrong baby girl? What happened?"

"Mike! Kim was right; he's been seeing Tracy this whole time. I feel like a complete fool!"

"I'm so sorry, Patrice." She lightly kissed me on my forehead and rocked me back and forth until my sobs completely stopped. We must've stood in the driveway for at least twenty minutes, until I couldn't cry anymore. I held my mother for strength, she whispered, "God has a plan for you, he's removing the old to bring in the new, let him do the work. I'll be here with you every step of the way." With those words I felt so much peace and had no more strength to shed another tear over Mike.

I helped my mom unpack all of the groceries and then headed upstairs to unwind in my room. My phone continued to ring, I wondered if it is one of the girls checking on me. It was Mike. It had been him the whole time blowing me up. I threw my phone. He was the last person that I wanted to talk to, and I simply wasn't strong enough to talk to him. The last thing I wanted to do was burst into tears over the phone. I wouldn't even give him the satisfaction. I took a long hot shower. My drama could wait one more day to be dealt with.

I wanted to jump out of my skin when the clock read 10:00 a.m. I never overslept. All of my crying must've drained me. I probably cried in my sleep. I heard the TV in the next room and assumed my mom was home too.

"Mom!"

"Yes. Patrice how do you feel this morning? Better, I hope because I have the whole day planned for us."

"Mom, why didn't you wake me up for school?"

"Because I realized that you needed to rest, and I didn't want you to face Mike today in school. You need some time to yourself, and one day isn't going to hurt. So, I scheduled a day for us at the spa to get a manicure and pedicure and then we can go shopping. Get dressed. I would like to leave here by 12 p.m." She didn't let me get a word in. Even though I had exams and homework assignments that were due, I looked forward to spending time with my mom, and, of course, the spa sounded great.

Responsible people go to work and school, so the spa wasn't too crowded. My mom and I had the whole spa to ourselves. It was very nice one that I hadn't been to before. There was a waterfall streaming down the wall, soft music playing, and a huge chandelier, which had dim lighting that reflected off of the paintings on the wall.

"Hello, welcome to Diamond Spa. How can I help you?"

"Yes, my daughter and I would like manicures and pedicures."

"Sure, pick a color. Someone will be right with you." I went with a French manicure, my usual. Two ladies walked out of the back to assist us, they looked very young, and I was hoping they would do a good job. Mom and I plopped into the plush leather chairs. I closed my eyes as the hot water bubbled around my legs. It felt like heaven.

"So how are you feeling today, Patrice?"

"I feel a whole lot better since yesterday, but it still hurts though."

"Those sort of things take time to heal. You and Mike spent a lot of time together. I liked Mike, but he wasn't for you. The best you can do is to start doing things you enjoy and continue to pray to God. Before you know it, he will be yesterday's news." I understood what my mom was saying. I knew she was being sympathetic, but it seemed so hard to completely get over him like that. I just couldn't believe he would lie to me. Once our pedicures finished, we walked over to the nail station.

"Would you like a massage as your get your nails done?"

"Of course," I said without hesitation. "I could definitely get used to this."

The mall parking lot was just as empty as the spa. We parked in the Bloomingdales lot and headed straight to the women's department. I grabbed a few shirts for school, along with a pair of jeans. As I sifted through the clothes, that fuchsia dress called for me again.

"Go get it," said Mom. "This is your day."

"Mom, are you serious that dress costs..."

"Like I said, this is your day. Let me worry about the cost." I must've floated to the dress. I didn't waste any time trying it on. It fit perfectly, even the sales girl admired from a distance. After my mom paid, we headed to get a slice of pizza, and we were home before we knew it. The day flew by and I had the best time, one that I would never forget. I felt great, and strong enough to face Mike in school tomorrow, and even more excited for the party that weekend.

I woke up before my alarm clock. I was still refreshed from the day before, and excited about the party. I did have a little nervous energy about seeing Mike in school, but looked forward to getting it over with. I smoothed my hair back into a ponytail, put on my silver hoop earrings, and applied my lip gloss. I was ready to go. Since my brother wasn't feeling well, he stayed home. I swear, that boy never missed a day of school. He must have really been sick. I hopped in my car and put the radio on full blast. *Girl on Fire* by Alicia Keys sounded through the speakers. I couldn't help but smile. I knew that today would be a good day.

For the first time in history, I got to school before the bell rang. My crew walked my way.

"Hey, girl, we've been calling you for days, where have you been!" I wanted to say mind your business, but I saw Tiffany was concerned.

"I'm sorry, I've been just laying low. I decided to take a day off yesterday and have some time to myself, but I'm back!"

"Cool...I know you weren't prepared for what you saw the other day in the mall, but I just wanted to let you know you can do so much better."

"Don't let no boy break your heart. It belongs to God." I didn't know Tiffany talked about God, but then I remembered her dad was a preacher. I would definitely need to talk to her, and meet her dad. I needed to get to know God a bit more.

I sat up front in all of my classes, especially my math class. I asked lots of questions, determined to do well on midterms. My teacher asked me to stay, which made me want to disappear. What on earth did he have to say to me?

"Patrice, you are doing very well young lady. Somebody has been studying. You aced the last exam we had. I didn't give the tests back because there is one student that still hasn't taken it, but I just wanted to let you know how you did. Keep up the good work." I wanted to hug Mr. Lewis, but decided to just thank him for the encouragement. I stayed up all night studying for it, I better have gotten good grade, I'm not going to bed at 3 a.m. for nothing.

My favorite girls saved a seat for me at lunch. I was happy to see that my favorite meal was being served: lasagna. The girls talked about the party and their outfits. Mike was peeking his head in from the hall, trying to get my attention. I knew this was the time to end it, but my lack of confidence was getting the best of me. All I wanted to do was run to my car, drive home, and dive into bed. But I knew this was the day. After all, I had everyone that ever motivated me cheering me on.

"I'll be back," I said to the girls.

"Patrice," said Amber. "Where are you going?" I stood up and blocked everything and everyone out around me. My focus was on was Mike, and what I had to say. He leaned in for a hug, and I quickly backed away.

"Whoa, what's that all about? I've been trying to call you and you don't answer my calls and I can't even get a hug?"

"Mike, I'll tell you what this is all about. It's about me finally realizing my value, and how I should be treated. It's about when you really love someone you wouldn't do anything to see them hurt, because if you did, it would hurt you. It's about telling the truth the first time because you wouldn't want to jeopardize a friendship. It's about me finding out who I am and finding out who you are: somebody who is not for me." I did it. It finally came out. Before I walked away, I turned to say one last thing: "by the way, you and Tracy look good together." With that I walked away with my head held high and a strut in my step. It felt good knowing what I deserved, to never settle for anything less.

That night at home I thought about my interaction with Mike, and would never forget the look on his face. He never saw me so strong, so confident. It had been some time since he saw me at all, and I had nothing but the best people pouring life in me when I needed it. I have to say I was shocked what was coming out of my mouth. I did feel good about letting go and finally facing the truth. They say that God won't put anything on you that you can't bear, and I was bearing this pretty well. With the quietness in my room, I was led to pray, there was no better time than this.

"God, I know I don't talk to you much, even though I'm always told that I should do it often. I want to get to know You better and want to know the plans that You have for me. I must admit, I'm hurt by what Mike did, but I refuse to look back. Can You please help me get over the pain? Amen."

The next morning, I woke up as refreshed as the day before. Instead of going through my normal routine, I went for a quick run. Running had been so therapeutic for me in the past, and I knew it would give me the boost of energy I needed. I ran a few times around the neighborhood and waved to a few neighbors. For some reason, they tried to stop me and have a conversation. I kept my pace and just said a simple good morning and enjoy your day. I never understood why someone would want to interrupt a work out.

I was happy to see my mom cooking a gourmet breakfast; she always knew what I needed. After getting dressed and taking some breakfast for the road, my brother and I talked about my trip with dad. He wanted to visit for the Christmas holiday. I thought it was a great idea; they didn't spend much time with each other. My brother reminded me so much of my dad, and they got along great. Desmond was doing well in basketball and football.

The school parking lot wasn't as full, pre-Christmas fever, where people were too busy shopping or hanging out with friends. I, on the other hand, couldn't afford to hang out. There were midterms to pass and my GPA to keep up. My brother and I hugged each other before parting ways. His buddies greeted him with a handshake, and girls stared at him in awe. He was popular, who knew?

There was a note on my locker, it said for me to come to the yearbook department. I was voted best dressed, and a photographer would be at the school next week to take my picture for that category. I was extremely flattered and surprised. I didn't know that people paid attention. I reread the memo until Tracy caught my attention. This was my first time seeing her since the fight. She didn't say anything to me, but she had the same glare she had from before. She was wearing Mike's sweatshirt. For some reason, I didn't feel any jealousy towards her, but I did feel sorry for her. I felt sorry because she didn't have a clue who she was, and for the first time, I was learning who I was and what I deserved.

My classes seemed to breeze by, maybe because the teachers were just as excited as we were for the weekend. I was even more excited; the party was tomorrow night. I had the outfit now, and all I needed was to get my hair done. I had my mom make me an appointment at this popular hair salon. I wanted the works.

After school, I headed straight to the packed salon. I didn't recognize any of the girls. I was glad that my stylist wasn't too busy, and that I would be her first client. Tina was in her twenties, and had been with the salon for about a year. She was always very stylish whenever I saw her. Today she had on a pair of black tights and an over sized cow neck sweater with red cowboy boots.

"Hey, Patrice! It's so good to see you. I saw your mom the other day, she said that you were doing great!"

"Yes, I am. How are you?"

"Girl, you know, the same old same old." I always wondered what that meant when people said that. It's disturbing to have nothing happen in your life.

"Oh, okay."

"So, what are we doing to your hair today?"

"I would like it curled."

"Oh, this style wouldn't be for the party tomorrow night will it? I hear everybody is going to be there."

"Yes, how did you know?"

"Girl, I work in a salon."

"Enough said."

"You might see me there." We both laughed.

After washing and blow-drying my hair, Tina curled my strands in the prettiest big curls. I was glad that I was getting it done the day before. I knew it would look even better the next day. When she finished, I gave her a tip along with the shampoo girl and made another appointment. I decided that I had to start taking better care of my hair, since it was long and hard to manage. I left when there were a lot more people coming in. I assumed it was for the party. It was becoming the talk of the town.

I reached home to my grandparent's car in the driveway. They didn't visit often, so when they did, it was such a nice surprise. We tended to visit their house more. As I burst in the house, my grandmother and grandfather gave me the biggest hug. I loved spending time with them. They were both filled with so much love. They were together for over forty years and still in love.

"Patrice, your hair is to die for." My grandmother always complimented me and it always made me feel good.

"Yes, baby girl," said Pop-Pop, they were both twirling me around. "You look stunning. What, you got a hot date?"

"No, Pop-Pop," I said, dizzy from spinning. "It's for a party that I'm going to tomorrow night."

"Well, you sure will be beating them boys with a stick, that's for sure."

"Patrice, you're growing up to be a beautiful young woman. I remember when you were a little crying baby, and now look at you. Are you dating anyone special?" I should've known that was the next question.

"No, Grandmom, I'm not dating anyone. I was, but I had to kick him to the curb."

"Baby girl, kick those boys to the curb and keep kicking those books. Patrice, I'm going to tell you what my mother used to tell me when I was your age. She used to say, 'don't ever lose yourself in a boy, lose yourself in God, He knows what's best for you. He will lead you to the one He has for you.'"

"Well, Grandmom, how will I know he's the one?"

"That's easy. No headaches. God is not the author of confusion."

"Well said, dear," Pop-Pop said. They sealed their words with a kiss. My grandparents were a portrait of true love.

After dinner I prepared for the party. My grandparents had me laughing the whole time at dinner. It was always nice spending time with family. My phone was ringing off the hook the whole night. My new crew must have all been thinking the same thing as me...p-a-r-t-y! I would call them back in the morning. Right now all I could think was about my outfit. My mom even bought me black pumps and gold hoop earrings. I was thinking about going to the mall to get my makeup done, but that would be doing too much.

"Patrice, telephone!"

"Desmond, can't you knock first! Who is it?"

"I don't know, I'm not your secretary! Where are you going with that dress?"

"A party. Tomorrow night."

"You are going to Reggie Smith's party, the star basketball player?"

"Yes, Desmond."

"Wow, I wish I could go, that has been the talk of the town. Is Mike going to be there?"

"I'm no longer with Mike. I thought you heard, nosey."

"Oh, I didn't know. Well, I know that I don't tell you this often, but you are beautiful and I always knew you could do better. Mike didn't deserve you." With that he closed my bedroom door. Tears welled in my eyes. I realized for the first time I believed I deserved better, too. When I went to answer the phone, no one was there. I thought it was strange, but didn't want to give it too much thought.

The next morning, I woke up with a crook in my neck. That is the last time I try to sleep like I'm Queen Elizabeth. I heard Mom vacuuming down stairs, and the whole house reeked of Pine-Sol. Vacuums should come with silencers, sleeping with that noise in the background is impossible.

"Hey, Patrice, do you want to go the mall?"

"Desmond, I really don't feel like it. I just woke up."

"Come on, I just want to get a pair of sneakers. We'll be in and out. Pleeease."

"All right, all right. Let me get dressed." I hated going to the mall on Saturdays. Lines were always too long and clothes always seemed picked over, but anything for my little brother. I couldn't go out looking crazy. You never knew who you might bump into.

I decided on my black bubble coat and Ugg boots. I wore my hair smoothed back in a ponytail, and fastened on hoop earrings. Ever since my brother got his permit, he had been begging us all for him to drive. I was a little hesitant at first, but thought what the heck. I knew what it felt like when wanting to drive. We pulled out of the driveway and it was smooth sailing to the mall. I was impressed with my little brother. He was maturing and already driving me around.

It took at least twenty minutes to find a parking space. We got inside and went our separate ways. We agreed to meet at the food court when we were done. I saw a few people from school who were shopping for the party. I even bumped into Tiffany; she said she'd been there for hours trying to find an outfit. She would pick me up at nine, which I was glad to hear. I really didn't feel like driving. I window shopped for a few more things and I glanced at my watch. It was already 1:30, an hour went by so fast. I was worried that Desmond had been sitting waiting for me, but when I arrived at the food court, he was with his friends eating pizza. He motioned me over to come sit with them.

"Hey, guys." My brother's friends were all very handsome. I knew they all would be heart-breakers when they got older.

"Patrice," one of his friends made room for me to sit. "Take a load off. Do you want something to eat?"

"No, I'm fine. I'll just take my brother's other slice."

"Patrice, I was going to eat that."

"Not anymore." His friends all started to laugh at our sibling bond.

"Hey, isn't that Mike and Tracy." This was the second time I saw them together, but the first time I saw Mike since the argument. I could tell he was nervous; he walked by with his hand in hers and couldn't even look at me. Tracy had a devilish grin, as if to say I told you so. Surprisingly, I didn't feel anything, I knew I was bigger than that, and it was my gain and her loss.

CHAPTER 10

Getting ready for the party was so exciting. I was ready to have a blast with the girls. I loved my outfit, my hair was falling just right, and to top it off, my mom let me borrow her clutch bag. When the horn blew, I dashed outside, but my mom called me back to give her a hug and kiss. Ever since Kim passed away, she'd been very affectionate, and constantly telling me how much she loved me.

"Patrice, I really wish you were driving your own car."

"Mom, don't worry. Tiffany is a very good driver. I'll call you when I get there okay?"

"Okay, baby, I love you."

"I love you too." Tiffany, Amber and Lisa looked great. We all wore dresses, very classy.

"You girls look so cute!"

"You do too, I see somebody went back and got that dress." Tiffany didn't miss a thing.

"My mom saw me eying it, and got it for me."

"Tell your mom I saw a dress I want in Bloomingdales." We all started to laugh. When we pulled up the long driveway, there were so many cars. The music pumped through the walls. I hoped the cops didn't get called tonight. We entered the mini-mansion and stood in the foyer in awe. There was a huge chandelier that sparkled as if it was made out of diamonds. Through the foyer there was a long winding staircase. There were marble floors throughout the house.

"Hi, girls, let me take your coats. Everyone is downstairs. I'm Reggie's aunt." She was nice. She gave us a tour of the house. Out back she said there was a pool and Jacuzzi and invited us back for the summer where there was sure to be another party. That was a party I wouldn't want to miss. Everyone danced and had a great time. Once our feet hit the floor we couldn't help but join in. I was so into the music and dancing with the girls that I didn't notice Reggie dancing in front of me.

"What's your name?"

"Patrice."

"Nice to meet you, Patrice, are you having a good time?!"

"Yeah."

"Are these your friends?"

"Yes, this is Tiffany, Amber, and Lisa."

"Nice to meet you," Tiffany said eating the snacks. "Great house."

"Thanks. If you ladies would excuse me, I have to greet more of my guests. Nice meeting you, Patrice."

"Girl, I think he likes you." Amber said while dancing.

"No, he doesn't. He was talking to all of us."

"Yes, but you didn't see how he was looking at you?"

"Well, so what. I didn't come here for that, I came to par-tay!" I must've danced to every song the DJ played. I was happy when the lights finally came on because my feet were screaming at me to sit down.

"I can't let the prettiest girl here leave without me walking her out." It was Reggie, I thought my heart would fall out of my chest. I was happy Mike saw that he wasn't the only one who moved on.

The next morning I felt like a complete zombie. I couldn't remember the last time I stayed up so late and danced so hard. I really enjoyed myself and promised I would hang out with the girls more often. For some reason, I couldn't get Reggie out of my mind. I knew it wasn't healthy to jump into another relationship, but I couldn't forget our dance, and he seemed like a pretty cool person. The blaring phone interrupted my daydream.

"Hello."

"Hey, girl, are you just getting up? It's after 11:00." Tiffany sounded bubbly every time I talked to her. She didn't know what sleep was.

"Yes, I am exhausted."

"We had so much fun last night. I saw you and Reggie dancing. Y'all looked so cute. Mike was looking hard, too."

"Good. He is yesterday's news."

"I'm glad to hear that. The reason why I was calling you is that my dad is having a Bible Study at my house tonight, I wanted to know if you would be interested to come?" I was curious how a Bible Study would have been, and I knew I wasn't going to church, and it would be nice to meet Tiffany's parents.

"Sure, I would love to."

When I pulled up to Tiffany's house, it proved what I only imagined. It was a long driveway that led to a huge white house with exposed brick and a four-car garage. There were so many windows; I could only imagine how beautiful it was during the day. When I rang the doorbell, a nice older lady answered and escorted me back to the Bible study session. It was packed with people from all different ages and ethnic backgrounds. There was a seat up front that I was a little nervous to take. I didn't want all of the attention. Since that's where I was being led, I slid in the seat quietly and joined in on the study.

"Thank you for joining us, you must be Tiffany's friend. I heard a lot about you. I'm Mr. Johnson, but you can call me Joe. We're currently in a series called 'Wholeness,' which we've been studying for a little over a week. Please feel free to join in on the discussion." I didn't really know what to add to the discussion, so I sat quietly and listened to the others.

"Well, Mr. Johnson," said Lisa. "Wholeness to me is being comfortable in your own skin, not caring what others think about you."

"Thanks, Lisa. Does anyone else want to add anything?"

"I think wholeness is loving yourself," said Tanya. "Loving every fiber of your being. Waking up in the morning and feeling complete."

"That's excellent Tanya. How about someone else? Any men in the room here tonight? What do you think wholeness is?"

"I think wholeness is having peace in your mind, body, soul, and spirit."

"Thanks, Shawn. Another excellent comment. The Webster dictionary defines wholeness as *mentally or emotionally sound.* All of you have mentioned very important components of wholeness, and each of you have to get to a level within yourselves and connect to God to achieve your ultimate capacity of wholeness. Wholeness equates Peace. Peace with God, and next: peace with yourself. If you don't have God in your life, then you are a person who lacks true peace."

"Mr. Johnson how do you have peace with God?" I couldn't believe those words left my mouth.

"Great question, Patrice. By spending time with Him everyday. He knows your thoughts. He knows your going and coming. He knew you before the foundation of this world. He is your creator and is concerned about you, whether you realize it or not. If you don't spend time with Him on a daily basis and you try to commune with Him, things may seem a bit off. It's just like a friend or relative, if you don't speak or spend time with each other, things may be a bit awkward at first because of the distance. It's the same with God. It's important that you don't let the distance or God seeming far away make you think He's not there. He's always there. You're never alone. Speak to Him. He's waiting for you. Everyone, this has been another great study. I look forward to seeing all of you next week."

After Bible Study, Tiffany showed me around the house. The living room was decorated in white and gold. I had never seen white leather furniture before. It was very classy underneath the huge pictures on the wall. I was sure those paintings had some significant meaning, and it looked like it cost lots of money, but I couldn't help but wonder why someone would pay so much for something that looked like a child's finger-paint project. After Tiffany showed me all of the family pictures, she escorted me up to her room. It was the size of an apartment. Her king size bed had a bright white comforter with crisp white sheets and about ten pillows for decoration. She also had a walk in closet that would put Beyoncé to shame.

"Tiffany, do you wear all of these clothes? I've never seen half of these outfits."

"No, not all of them. My mom likes to shop, so every now and then she picks me up something that she thinks I will like."

"Wow, you must be very happy living in this big ole' house. You seem to have everything you want."

"Yeah, I guess that's what people think, but none of it makes me happy. I guess I'm so used to having nice things, it doesn't make me feel anything to be honest with you. Lately, I've been having an empty feeling, and I'm not sure why. My mom has noticed, and she's been on a rampage trying to cheer me up. We go and get our nails done, the newest handbag, she's even took me to look at cars. None of it seems to matter. I need something deeper to feel this void." I know if I had a closet like that, I would be happy for life. Whatever void she was feeling, I hoped it would soon be filled.

I got home exhausted. It seemed like my mom and brother were too. Their doors were closed and the lights were off.

"Patrice, is that you? How was Bible Study?" My mom was half sleep, but she always slept light until I was in the house.

"It was nice, I learned a lot. I may go again. Tiffany lives in a huge house, but she said that she feels empty at times. I never met anyone who had everything but wasn't happy."

"You'll realize, baby girl, that money will never buy happiness. There is something deeper that will give you joy and peace."

"What is it?"

"He lives on the inside of you, baby: God." With that, I closed her door and went to bed. I don't remember falling asleep, but I did sleep peacefully thinking about my mom's words.

I must have overslept. I woke up with my clothes on. My alarm didn't go off; then I remembered I didn't set it. I was tempted to stay home, but it was the last day to kick off Christmas vacation, and I also had an exam in the afternoon. I dashed into the shower and threw on my most comfortable sweatpants, sweatshirt, and boots. I wondered where my brother was, but then realized my mom took him to the doctor's because his cold wasn't getting any better.

I got to school in the middle of first period, my Broadcast News class, but didn't care much. I knew I was getting an A. As soon as I pushed the door opened to the class, everyone stopped what they were doing. You would have thought I was the president.

"Nice of you to join us, Queen Patrice." I didn't know why the teacher was always so sarcastic. She was much too old to try to argue with me.

"I'm sorry I'm so late. I got a late start."

"No need for an explanation, just find a seat and review your assignment on the board." The assignment was to interview someone you looked up to. It had to be a sit down interview and the questions to ask would be based on that person's profession and background. I was excited about this project because I knew whom exactly I would interview: Tiffany's dad. I learned a lot from him at Bible Study, and I knew he had so much more to share. Since the assignment was due after Christmas, I knew there was a lot of time to complete it. Now I just had to ask her dad if he would like to be on camera.

After first period I bumped into Reggie. He was on his way to class wearing a sweatshirt and sweatpants. I didn't remember him being so tall, definitely, cuter than I remembered.

"Hey, Patrice. How is it going? What have you been up to since the party?"

"Nothing much. Just hanging out with friends and getting much needed rest."

"I hear that. I will be throwing another party on New Year's Eve, and would love for you to come."

"Sure, I'll be there." That's all that I could think of to say.

"I'm glad you can make it. I have to get to class."

"Okay." There was so much more I wanted to say like, "How was your weekend? What are you doing this weekend?" I didn't expect to see him, but I was glad I did.

I spent second period in the library studying for my upcoming math test. I felt confident about it. A couple of kids in the class asked for my help. They all knew I was serious about my grades.

After going through a few math problems, it was time for lunch. I met Tiffany alone since the girls were taking exams. I chewed on a sandwich while Tiffany picked at her lunch from home. Since I've known her, I've never seen her buy school lunch.

"So did you hear about Reggie's upcoming New Year's Eve party?"

"Yes, I saw him walking to class after first period. He invited me."

"Really? I knew he liked you."

"I'm not sure if he does, but it's not something I'm focusing on now."

"I understand, there are too many other things, like college. My parents are on me about completing my college applications. The deadline is coming up soon." I was putting my own applications on the back burner. I was supposed to visit NYU over the holiday thanks to Mrs. Washington coordinating a meeting with a recruiter. I also had to think about what I would write in my college essay.

I breezed through my math test, as usual. I was the first one to leave, and felt the rest of the class staring a hole through me as I exited the class. I wish I could give them the answers, but I helped as much as I could, it was up to them now. Since I completed the test early, I went to visit Mrs. Washington. I needed some advice on writing my college essay. The secretary let me right in. Mrs. Washington was typing on the computer and welcomed me with a smile.

"Patrice, this is a pleasant surprise. How are your classes?"

"Classes are fine. I just had a math test and I finished early."

"Well, that's great. You must be studying hard. Do you plan to visit NYU? I've spoken to my contact there, and they're looking forward to meeting you."

"Yes, my mom will be purchasing my flight this weekend. We will be going over the holiday."

"That's wonderful, let me know how you like it."

"The reason why I stopped by is my college essay, I was

wondering if you could give me some pointers?"

"The main point I will give you, my dear, is to speak from your heart. What do you want that person reading your essay to know about you? Why should they accept you into their school? Dig deep into yourself and show the beauty you exude inside and out on to the page." With Mrs. Washington's advice, I knew exactly what I would write about. I knew that this essay and with my grades would get me in. I was happy that Mrs. Washington saw such beauty in me, even though I didn't feel beautiful. *How do I feel beautiful?*

On my way on home, I thought a lot about Kim. She should have been here to share graduation and go to college with me. We had so many plans together and share our lives. Life seemed to go away within a blink of an eye. Since she wasn't here, I wanted to do everything I could to make her proud. I was excited to visit NYU, and didn't know what to expect. I had never been on a college campus before. I was glad my mom was going with me to help make the decision. I would be taking my SATs in the morning, and was confident I would do well. After all, I'd been prepping since I started high school.

Mike had gone from my mind. Other priorities had taken hold. I still couldn't believe he was lying about Tracy the whole time. Why couldn't he just tell me the truth? I guess I would never know, and at this point I no longer cared as much.

When I got home the house smelled like cookies. My mom loved baking over the holidays, she even had the biggest Christmas tree she could find shining bright in the living room. I remember as a child decorating the tree as a family, but it was something my brother and I grew out of.

"I see you're in the Christmas spirit."

"Yes, and I have all of your favorites. Chocolate chip, oatmeal raisin, peanut butter crunch, and lemon. I also have a cake in the oven."

"Thanks. So what cookies are you making for Desmond I said with a smile."

"Oh, Patrice now you know you can't eat this by yourself," she laughed. "I wanted to wait for you and Desmond to help decorate, but you know how it is to get both of you in the house at the same time. So I went ahead and did it myself. It's my day off. Oh, and I got our tickets to visit NYU. Have you worked on your essay yet?"

"No, I haven't."

"Well, have it done before we leave. It's one last thing you have to worry about. Besides, we're going to be there anyway. I'm really looking forward to visit the campus. My baby girl is going to college." I went up to my room, listening to my mom reminisce about when I was a baby and her getting all mushy was the last thing on my agenda after a day of school. I needed to write my essay, but didn't know where to begin. I had to start somewhere, so *I just started typing...*

As a little girl, I always dreamed of going to college. I have always enjoyed learning and, most of all, reading. I read as many books as I could get my hands on. Sometimes even falling asleep with books in my bed. Although I had a thirst for knowledge, I struggled in finding who I was and what I was meant to do on this earth. I analyzed myself subconsciously through friends, or through a boyfriend, but deep down there was always a void that no one could fill. I appreciated people like my principal, Mrs. Washington, for believing in me, and my mother who taught me that life is a journey, you won't have everything figured out all at once, but to always enjoy the journey you're on.

My journey shall continue, while, sadly, my best friend's journey has come to an end, due to a fatal car accident. We shared lifelong dreams together, and promised we would attend the same college. She was beautiful, full of personality and life. She inspired me to be better. I never would've guessed in a million years that she would be gone from me. Though one life has ended, my life will be just beginning, and as I embark on a new adventure in my college career, NYU is the place where I would like to start that journey. There will always be unanswered questions, but the void will continue to close as I blossom with wisdom and confidence, as I learn what I was born to be.

I have been very active in my Broadcast News program in high school, and hope I can carry what I have learned into your program. I know that college will not be all fun and games, but preparation for adulthood, and to experience independence in the real world. Since I have lived at home all of my life, this will be a huge eye opening experience for me. One that I must admit is a little scary, but a road that I must travel.

I have learned that life is never promised, but even so, life is to be lived and pursue dreams. Since my friend will never have that opportunity to do so, I choose to live my life and pursue every dream ahead of me. Her death has taught me to never fear and cherish friends and family. The last words she spoke on this earth were that she loved me. I loved her too. I still love her, and most of all, I'm learning to love myself. From this point on, I will be living life for the both of us, and I know that she is proud, cheering for me from heaven. It is my hope that I may have the opportunity to grace your stage on graduation day and accept my degree in preparation for my next journey in life, one that will be on purpose and in reach of my destiny...that destiny begins at NYU.

Sincerely,

Patrice Johnson

Finally finished. There were so many bottled up feelings about Kim, it all came out on paper. I never planned on including Kim in the essay. I was pleased how it turned out, it reflected who I was, and what I wanted to become. I just hoped to be accepted. There were only a few months until graduation. I wondered what college Mike was going to, and if he ever thought about me. I was starting to miss him, the more I thought about him. I dozed off to sleep and silenced my mind of all the noise of my life.

CHAPTER 11

—ɯ—

"**P**atrice! Wake up, it's time to take your SAT test. You can't be late!" I always told myself that I never needed an alarm clock, my mom was the best alarm clock I ever had.

"Mom, I'm coming!" This was the day to ignore fashion. I had to be at the school by 7 a.m., and the only thing I wanted was a cup of hot tea and my favorite hooded sweatshirt. It didn't take me long to get ready. My mom already had a raisin bagel and my hot tea waiting on the kitchen table. I scarfed down as much as I could and sprinted to my car.

Luckily, there were still people coming in as I slid into my seat. I wasn't sure why I was so nervous. I've been taken tests my whole life. Maybe it was because this was the first test colleges see, this exam helps decide on acceptances. Maybe it was because the test was timed, and I always liked to check over my answers. I said a quick prayer and next I heard:

"You may begin."

There were numerous stories that I had to read and chronologically put in order. Of course there were those math questions even Einstein couldn't answer. I did the best I could and felt confident in achieving a decent score. As I walked my test up to the staff, I noticed Tracy in the back staring blank at the test. I had no idea she planned on going to college. I wondered where she planned on attending. While I walked passed her desk, she glanced up at me with a smirk. I smiled back at her, my letting her know I had moved on. Walking to my car I felt great. I was through with the SATs and ready to do something exciting for the weekend. I crossed the street. Reggie waved me over to his car in the parking lot.

"Hey, Patrice, over here!" I instantly wanted to bolt to my

car and pretend that I didn't see him. I looked horrible, like I just rolled out the bed, which is exactly what I did. I dreaded him seeing me like this, but I had no choice but to face him. Hopefully, he would remember how I looked at his party.

"Hi, Reggie," I said, as if I didn't care to see him.

"I guess you just finished your test. How do you think you did?"

"Fine, I guess. I'm just glad it's over."

"I agree. I wonder why they ask questions that you will never use once you're out of school. I think there all trick questions." We both laughed.

"So, what do you have planned for the rest of the day?"

"I was actually just thinking about that. I want to do something fun, anything to get my mind off of that test."

"Well, how about you take a ride with me?"

"When?"

"Now. Unless you have other plans."

"No, it's not that. It's just that I would have to go home and change."

"For this adventure, you don't need to get all fancy, besides you look beautiful."

"Let's go." Hearing that I was beautiful felt amazing. I didn't care what I had on, now I wanted to know where he was taking me.

Reggie drove on the expressway. He expressed how he felt leaving high school and going off to college. He was sure on getting picked up by the NBA, but said that he had to finish college before going pro. I was surprised he didn't enjoy high school. He was popular, especially among the girls.

"People think that my life is perfect because I play ball but it's not. They don't realize I'm up most of the time at 6 a.m. practicing sun up to sun down on weekends. Since my dad played, he knows how important practice is, there's always someone out there trying to perfect their game. I have to be better than the next guy. Basketball is my life right now."

"So, have you dated any girls at all? I did hear about Tina, is it true that you were in a relationship?"

"Yes, we were in a relationship, but it didn't last long. She didn't understand what it took dating someone like me. She wanted me to take her out a lot, but I couldn't. I'm either practicing or preparing for a game. She just wanted more than I could give.

"So, how about you Ms. Wendy Williams? You dated Mike for awhile."

"Yeah, well not anymore. He's now with Tracy. He never told me he was seeing her behind my back."

"Wow, well that's too bad. I didn't know. I'm sorry. We play ball together, but we're not too close. I had no idea that he was dating Tracy."

"Well if it means anything, you are very beautiful and you deserve nothing but honesty and respect." We pulled into this huge parking lot. There was a sign blinking, lights that read Race To The Finish Line. We were at a racecar track. I loved racing cars, and it was something different. I had not done this in a long time.

"See, I told you that you were dressed perfectly." We got our helmets, the same color as the car we were ready to drive.

"Are you thirsty? I'm going to get us a soda."

"Sure," I screamed over the blaring motors. He came back with two cherry cokes.

"Let's make a toast."

"A toast?"

"Yes, a toast to us. New friends." I raised my cup and clinked our drinks. We cheered to new friends.

It was our turn to step into our race cars. I strapped on my helmet. The crew went to each car to make sure everyone was buckled in safely. We sat in the car, waiting for the flag to raise. My adrenaline raced through my body. I couldn't believe I was about to drag race the star basketball player. Before I could think a second thought, the flag raised and the horn blared. It was my time to floor the gas. I wanted to win. I drove the car as fast as I could, but couldn't seem to catch up to Reggie, he must've been going two hundred miles per hour. As he flew past the finish line, I slowed down, knowing I left the others in the dust. I was happy at least I came in second place.

"That was so much fun!" I couldn't stop laughing like a child!

"It was fun. Sorry I had to beat you like that."

"At least I came in second."

"That you did, I'm proud of you." He then put his arm around me, and I never wanted him to let go.

The school parking lot was empty. I couldn't believe how much time flew by. I knew mom was going crazy, wondering where I was. I meant to call her at the race track, but was too excited to speak.

"Thank you for taking me to the race track. I had a really good time."

"The feeling is mutual. Maybe we can do it again some time soon. Don't forget my New Year's Eve party, I hope to see you there."

"I wouldn't miss it."

Driving home, my thoughts were racing a mile a minute. It did feel good receiving such attention. I wondered why it felt good, when I received attention from a guy. Why didn't I feel whole just being by myself? Why did I need a boyfriend to be happy? The more I thought about my self-worth, the more I became even more confused. I was happy to see all of the lights in the house when I pulled up. I was dying to tell my mom about the day.

"Mom!"

"Back here, Patrice!" My mom was still cooking and baking, she was always in a good mood around this time of year. She probably didn't notice how long I was gone.

"Hey, baby, how was the test?"

"It was long, boring, and I'm glad it's over with."

"Well, I'm glad too. What did you do after the test? It's past eight. You know I hate when you stay out late and I don't know where you're at."

"That's what I'm so excited to tell you. I was with the star basketball player, Reggie Smith. He took me to a race track. I had a really good time."

"Reggie Smith!" I swear my brother had ears of a cat. "You

were with Reggie Smith, now that's more like it."

"Well, I would like to meet this Reggie since he's taking my daughter out."

"Okay, I'll introduce you." As I tried to rush out of the kitchen to avoid a lecture she had already began her speech.

"Patrice, I understand that you want to date, and when you go to college I'm sure you will be interested in someone, but I really want you to be comfortable in your own skin. I want you to focus on loving yourself before you decide to try to love someone else. Every day you must wake up and know you can conquer anything you set your mind to, that you don't need any boy to make you happy. Be happy just being you." I thought my mom must've been reading my mind. I didn't want to be like the other girls in the school always wanting a boyfriend or crying over a broken heart. I really wanted to find me.

I must've been exhausted because I woke with the phone blaring in my ear at 8 a.m. I always had a rule: never talk before eight on Saturday. To avoid one more shrieking ring, I answered.

"Hello..." I barely recognized my own sleepy voice.

"Hi, Patrice, I am sorry to call you so early. This is Tracy. I'm probably the last person you want to talk to. I got your number from Mike, well not directly. I really need to talk to you. I don't have anyone else to talk to. I know this seems weird but..."

"Is everything alright?"

"Yes, but it would help if I had someone to talk to. Is there any way you can swing by my house later? I can give you my address."

"Uhhhh...I guess. Sure. I can be there in a few hours. What is the address?"

"534 Alberts Lane."

"Okay, I'll see you soon."

I couldn't imagine what Tracy had to talk to me about. She sounded upset. Tracy was the last person I wanted to see, but I was curious by her mysterious phone call. I was even more curious to see where she lived, I can be a little nosey.

Since it was pouring rain, I wore something comfortable: sweat pants, a hooded sweat shirt, and running sneakers.

"Mom, I will be back shortly."

"Okay, be careful out there," she screamed from the kitchen. "Roads are slippery." If she knew where I was going, she would have forbidden my departure. That was one thing my mom couldn't stand, drama.

I drove the wet roads to Tracy's and thought nothing but the worst. What if her friends were there to jump me? I mean I did give her a pretty bad beat down in front of everyone at school. Maybe she's embarrassed and wants to get me back? What if Mike is there? And all she wants is to throw their relationship in my face? Whatever the reason, I was sure to find out soon.

The houses on Alberts Lane were run down. There were boys on the corner hanging out playing loud music. I saw police cars chasing two guys. I never saw so much action in one place. If my mom knew I drove here alone, she would kill me, if I got out of this alive, that is. I found Tracy's house, the lot with the long grass behind a rusted gate. There was an older lady sitting on a porch smoking a cigarette.

"Hi, baby, are you here to see Tracy? She's right inside. Aren't you precious."

"Thank you." The floor inside creaked with every step. It was dark. There was someone watching TV, someone else asleep on the couch. Back in the kitchen there was a girl cooking and two kids on the floor playing board games. The walls had pictures of Tracy and her mom when she was little.

"Patrice," Tracy was walking down the stairs.
"Thank you so much for coming. Did my brother even offer you something to drink? Tony, you could have at least got up and offered her some water or something. All you do is watch that TV." Tony never turned his head, mesmerized by the picture on the screen. "Well, you can come upstairs to my room. Would you like some juice or something?"

"No, I'm fine." Once, upstairs in her room it was very neat. Her bed was made and I noticed her clothes and shoes in her huge closet. Tracy was always nicely dressed and I was unsurprised by how organized she was.

"Patrice, I know we haven't been friends, but you were the only person that I could call. I know you don't want to hear me vent about Michael, but it's deeper than that. It just seems like you've gotten over him so fast while I'm so miserable with him. I really thought that it would be great being with the star basketball player and going to all of the games and everyone knowing me as his girlfriend, but you've already lived that life and you seemed to let it go just like that. I know he's a cheater, but I still can't find the strength to let go. This may seem so crazy, but I wish I had the courage you have. You are so happy, and I'm not."

I really didn't know what to say. There were rumors about Michael seeing one of the cheerleaders, but I didn't know how true it was. Listening to Tracy reminded me so much of myself, of that longing to feel wanted and needing to be in a relationship, and quite honestly, I still struggled with that void. I was still healing over Michael.

"Tracy, I'm really caught off guard by all of this. I still can't believe that you would call me and invite me over your house to talk about my ex-boyfriend. We haven't even been broken up for six months. The whole time we were in a relationship, you were talking to him behind my back, and every time you would see me in school all you would do is make smart comments or stare a hole through me. You plotted for my boyfriend the whole time!" I felt myself getting more angry by the second. I wanted so badly to grab her by the neck, but I had to calm down.

"You just have nerve calling me. I should have never come here! Good luck with having my seconds." I reached for the door. Tracy must have been very desperate for advice or just crazy, she grabbed my shoulder as I tried to leave.

"Patrice, please don't go!" As tears streamed down her face, I knew that this moment was bigger than me, this was some-one very depressed reaching out for help. "I truly didn't mean to hurt you, it may seem strange, but I always admired you. I always thought you were very pretty. You always dress nice, and you have always seemed super confident. Everything I want to be."

"So you admired me so much that you decided to go after my boyfriend?"

"It wasn't like that at all. We actually had a few classes together and became study partners with other classmates. He talked about you all the time, and it is true that I found that attractive. We became friends and I developed feelings for him, not knowing that he would do the same thing to me that he did to you. It's gotten to the point I don't know who I am anymore. I feel so empty. I cry all the time. Being with Mike was supposed to make me happy, but in the end I feel so miserable." Listening to Tracy showed me that she was empty going into the relationship; I knew because I felt that feeling of emptiness and loneliness prior to my relationship with Michael. I held on, thinking that it would get better. I watched those tears stream down her face, and instead of anger I felt compassion for someone that resembled myself. I wanted to say so much, but the only thing I could do is wrap my arms around her.

"If you wouldn't mind," I said. "I would like for you to come to church with me. The pastor is awesome and I'm sure you will get something from it."

"Sure," she said, and broke into soft sobs, holding me tight.

I couldn't believe Tracy was going to church with me. I could hardly believe I was in her house. I didn't even want to be friends with her. I actually liked how things were, seeing each other and not speaking. I'd be happy if we never spoke. What if Mike saw us together and thought that I was trying to break them up? The last thing I needed was Mike calling me.

I pulled into my driveway. Mom and Desmond were sitting on the porch.

"Hey, Patrice, where have you been?"

"You wouldn't believe where I came from. I just left Tracy's house."

"Tracy! The girl you beat up?!" My brother was just as shocked as I was.

"Yes, that Tracy. She called me early this morning and

needed to talk. She was actually venting about Mike and knows he is cheating on her. She admired the way I moved on and wanted my advice. Weird, huh?"

"No, that's not weird at all. You never know whose watching you and who you're an inspiration to. Your life could help her get out of an unhealthy situation. God works in mysterious ways, you thought you would be enemies for life but could end up being very close friends."

"Friends!" Desmond's face pinched into a snarl. "Patrice, you should never be that girl's friend. Beat her up just one more time. I don't like that girl, anybody who messes with my sister...

"We know: messes with you." We all busted out in laughter.

The next morning I called Tracy to make sure she was still coming to church. She was already dressed and getting a ride from her mom. I put on a purple skirt and a black turtle neck sweater and black boots. My heaviest coat was needed; it was always freezing this time of year. I hitched a ride to church with my mom and brother, which I never do, I'm always the late one. Once we reached the church I noticed Tracy and her mom walking inside.

"There she goes!"

"Wow, aren't you excited now that you're best friends," my brother said.

"Be quiet, we are not."

"That's good she decided to bring her mom," my mom said. We gathered inside, there was still plenty of room next to Tracy. I slid in and my mom and brother followed. I adjusted in my seat. Tracy leaned over and gave me a tight hug. There was such a peace in the atmosphere; I gave her a smile. The choir sang a few hymns that made Tracy teary eyed. It wasn't long before the pastor stood at the podium and greeted the visitors.

"I am excited for all of you that are visiting on this day. I hope that you all come back and visit us again. Today, it has been on my heart to talk about filling the God-Size Void. Many people live their whole lives searching for things to fill the voids in their hearts. They enter into relationships where there is no happiness, a black hole of emptiness. They buy new houses, new cars, take exotic vacations, but still as empty as before. Why you ask? It's a void that only God can fill. He is waiting for you to seek Him. He wants to fill that longing in your heart. I feel like I'm talking to someone today. Young girls, stop chasing after these boys. You were not created to chase anything. God made you beautiful in His image. Stop. Stop trying to make these boys notice you with revealing, tight clothes. Your beauty alone is enough. You were created for just one Adam not twenty. Let that Adam find you, let him court you, and never let a man equate sex with love. *'Love is patient, love is kind, it is not easily angered, it does not boast, it does not envy. Love is not deceit.'* Young ladies, stop trying to force a young man to be the one. Don't be afraid to let go. Learn to give these young men their wings and fly away, and if he's not the one, you should never want him to fly back."

I couldn't believe that the very thing that I've been through and what Tracy was going through would actually be preached this very day. Tracy kept squeezing my hand. We went from enemies to slowly becoming friends. Once the service ended, I took Tracy to greet the pastor. He was a very tall, slender man, very distinguished, grey beard, and black glasses. He greeted us both with an enormous smile.

"Hello, young ladies. What are your names?"

"Patrice," I said above a whisper.

"I'm Tracy."

"Well, it's lovely to meet you.

I wanted to say that I enjoyed your sermon but he continued to speak.

"So I imagine you young ladies will be graduating and will soon be off to college. You are at a very critical stage in life, learning about yourself, full of curiosity about the world. Always continue to have a thirst for knowledge, continue to be curious, and most importantly know thyself, and continue to seek God with all your heart and mind. He is the source."

It took a while for Tracy and I to move out the way. He had already started his council. We were completely paralyzed by his words and probably both thinking the same thing. How do we know ourselves and how do we get to the source? As Tracy and I walked our separate ways in a parking lot. We gave each other one last hug and promised to call each other over the holiday. Although Tracy enjoyed the service, and I felt sorry for what she was going through, I still didn't want her to get too close. I didn't want her telling Michael my business.

I was happy to sleep in Monday morning. Christmas vacation was finally here. I loved this time of year, two weeks off of school. I was also excited for Reggie's New Year's Eve Party. Since my mom and I would be traveling to NYU in a few days, I packed for the trip. There was a tug at my heart, soon I would no longer be staying in my room or coming home every day after school. I was to be a college student, and honestly, I was scared to death. I was scared that I wouldn't meet new friends, scared that I may not do well in class, and just plain scared of being so far away from home. Although I was afraid, I had to confront those fears, and move on to the next chapter. My mom had the same idea, packing and doing laundry. She was always prepared.

"Patrice, I'm finished packing. Is there anything else you want me to pack in my bag?"

"Yes, maybe a few. I'm going to finish my packing today. Can we visit Grandmom and Pop-Pop? They won't be here for the holiday."

"We can go together, that was on my agenda for the day anyway. Be ready by noon." This was the coldest time of year. My suitcase mainly consisted of sweaters, jeans and Uggs. For my admissions interview, I decided to wear a black suit with white button up shirt. I've always loved that look. It always looked so professional. I zipped my suitcase when reality dawned on me. I would soon be a college student.

I was looking forward to spending time with my grandparents. Their love had conquered so much, and they both were full of such wisdom. I knew I would hear exactly what I needed in order to conquer the fears of college.

I was ready at exactly 12 p.m., and my mom had her coat

on. My brother stayed home alone, any chance he got to have the house to himself he took full advantage of.

As we drove through the snow filled streets, I cherished the few times spent in the car with my mother. Our lives had been so busy traveling here and there, that we missed what was going on in each others' lives. I enjoyed the quiet moments, the moments where we said nothing at all. We reached my grandparents house. Grandmom was just arriving home. She was spunky, not one that you can keep in the house, even in bad weather.

"Grandmom, where are you coming from?"

"Patrice, I didn't know you were coming over." I always loved to watch her face light up when she saw me. It was as if I was the only one on the planet.

"I had to go to the grocery store to pick up a few things. You know nothing can keep this granny down." It was true. We both had to laugh. We entered the house. The smell of cookies smacked us in the face. Even if nothing was in the oven, something always smelled sweet. My grandfather was always sitting in his favorite chair watching the news.

"College girl," he said. "What do I owe the honor to be in your presence this afternoon?"

"Pop-Pop, I'm not a college girl yet."

"Well, in my book you are. I always knew you would go to college. Come on over here and sit down and tell me what's going on with you." As a little girl I hated when my grandfather would want to have heart to heart talks, especially if it was about boys, but now I couldn't wait. He always made me feel like I could do anything, and he was always interested in what I had to say.

"Well, in a few days I will be visiting NYU. My school principal has a good friend in admissions and thought that it would be a great school for me to attend."

"This will be a great milestone in your life. Remember that your journey as an individual is one that you have to walk alone. You will make mistakes and sometimes you may fall, but always get back up. Fear paralyzes you. You always want to continue moving, continue to have goals and accomplish them. Without goals you are sitting still, and when you are sitting still you are bored, and as good as paralyzed. God planted too many gifts inside of you to share with the world to sit still. Always remember that sweetheart. Now you know what I'm going to ask you next right?" I had to laugh. Our conversation never ended without a discussion on who I was dating. I had a crush on Reggie, but didn't want to mention his name. My grandfather pulled it out of me.

"Oh, you have your eye on somebody. Come on who is it?"

"It's a guy named Reggie, he's on the basketball team."

"A basketball player!?" My grandmother screamed from the kitchen. She always managed to involve herself in every conversation.

"Yes, a basketball player. We only went out once. I'm going to his New Year's Eve Party."

"Well, honey," my grandfather pursed his lips and squinted his eyes. There was intent on his face. "These are the best years of your life. Enjoy every moment. You will never be able to get this time back. I know you like this guy, but always take your time in getting to know a person. Never feel the need to rush in a relationship. Always let things flow naturally, never force anything."

"Your grandfather is right," my grandmother brushed my hair with the back of her hand. "Never rush into anything. You are a beautiful girl, and you have to know it in your heart. One of the greatest things that you can do for yourself at this exciting time in your life is getting to know yourself. You see, when you know yourself, you are not easily swayed by wanting to be loved or filling an empty void in your life. Learn how to love on yourself, and you will go through life with a lot less heartache. Now, help me set the table. Dinner is ready."

It was a complete feast. My grandmother cooked baked chicken, rice, rolls, macaroni and cheese, string beans, sweet potatoes, and for dessert her famous baked apple pie. They loved telling stories about when my mom was a little girl. I always felt warm when I visited my grandparents, and I knew that was the first place I would go to during college breaks.

After washing dishes and more jokes about the old days, my mom and I got ready to leave. My mom was sad, but didn't say anything. I knew she wasn't ready for me to leave home. If she only knew I wasn't ready to leave home either.

There was only one more day before leaving for NYU. I spent the day shopping with the girls. We wouldn't be spending any time together next year. Tiffany had already been accepted to Georgetown University, her family's alma mater. Lisa was accepted to Harvard. She was in every gifted program. Amber planned on attending Yale. We were all going to be spread out. There was always homecomings and holidays. The first call to action was to plan our senior week vacation to Miami.

The music was so loud in Tiffany's car. I could barely hear myself talk. She finally lowered the volume after screaming every word.

"So, how are you and Mr. Reggie? I can't wait to go to his party!"

"Yeah, that would be nice. I don't see Reggie too often because of basketball. He's busy. He did take me to the go carts after the SAT test. That was fun."

"Wow! I didn't know y'all were spending time. We definitely have to catch up." I smiled, it wasn't at all what Tiffany was trying to make it out to be. A lot of the girls wanted to be in relationships. Since Mike, my focus has been on college and graduating.

The mall was packed due to Christmas break. Lisa and Amber were engulfed in conversation standing outside of the Gap.

"Hey, girls," Tiffany yelled out the car window while blaring the horn, scaring everyone that walked by. We found parking that might as well have been miles from the mall, and joined the shopping chaos. We must have went into every store, stopping every so often to talk to others from school. Lisa and Amber definitely came to shop for clothes. They had bags full. They had outfits for Reggie's New Year's Eve Party. Tiffany wanted to wait for when I came back from NYU to get our dresses.

I bumped into Tracy at the food court. It was bound to happen. I was happy to see her even though we haven't talked since church.

"Tracy! How are you? I've been meaning to call you but things have been so busy." I rambled and noticed she didn't have that same after-church glow. There was a sadness that I had never seen before. I tried to cheer her up when Mike came walking over. It was as if I had seen a ghost. He was uncomfortable, barely acknowledging me.

"Come on, baby, are you ready? They didn't have the sneakers I was looking for." Tracy noticed the blank look on my face, and all of the unsaid things that only she would know what I was thinking.

"Tracy, can I speak with you in private for a minute?" I had no idea why those words left my mouth, and I didn't care what Mike was thinking. All I had were questions. All I wanted was answers.

"What do y'all have to talk about," Mike said.
"Man, I don't even care. Just hurry up." Tracy walked with me to the bathroom. I let the questions fly.

"Tracy, I don't understand. What are you doing with Mike after all you shared at your house? Why did you come to my church? Why did you share so much with me about your feelings and the unhealthy relationship? I don't want you to get the wrong idea, I don't want to be with him. Believe me. I'm just having a hard time understanding why you would be with someone who you don't trust and is constantly hurting you." Tracy broke down and cried. I didn't feel sorry for her. I didn't even want to wrap my arms around her. I was angry.

"Patrice," she said through tears. "I'm not like you. You are so strong and beautiful. I can't leave him, he's all I have."

"You are right. You're not like me. You are Tracy, and you are beautiful. You are smart, fun, and deserve the best. You have to believe that within yourself. What are you going to do when he goes away to college? Do you really think he's going to stay with you? What if you get pregnant? Anything can happen." I was getting upset myself. It wasn't my life, but I felt like I was trying to save hers.

Tracy just stood there with a blank look, as if she didn't hear me and said under a whisper, "I have to go."

CHAPTER 12

—⁊⁊—

It was time to visit NYU. We made it through the traffic just in time to the airport. Once we received our boarding passes, we stood in the security line, which seemed to go into eternity. Traveling over the holiday will surely test your patience. We reached the gate to our boarding plane. I was happy in my comfortable clothes, I planned on sleeping for the entire flight. My mom talked a lot about Desmond. She was so worried about him staying home, even though my grandmom would be there to check in on him. I did a lot of thinking about Tracy and her decision to stay with Mike. I could only pray that she would get the strength she needed, the strength I had found.

"We are now descending into New York. It is partly cloudy and thirty degrees. Thank you for choosing Delta Airlines."

It seemed that I was only sleep for ten minutes. We claimed our bags and hopped into a cab. Time Square was beautiful. I was always amazed by the many lights and countless tourists taking pictures. As cars zoomed passed people running after cabs, I wondered how I would fit in the big city of New York. The hotel was decorated so beautifully, a huge Christmas tree in the lobby, and friendly staff.

"This is where I will be staying when I come to visit you."

"Mom, I haven't even visited the campus yet."

"Patrice, if they can offer some sort of scholarship there isn't a choice in the matter unless you plan on getting a job." My mom was always good in snapping me out of my fantasy world.

"What a blessing it would be if you can attend this school. It would surely look great on your resume." There wasn't too much time to explore the city. I had an early morning meeting with Ms. Turner, head of admissions. I had my college application and essay.

I felt ready, but my stomach cart wheeled.

I felt so small on campus the next morning. Everyone knew how to get to their classes without getting lost. I would constantly be late to all of the classes and find it extremely hard building relationships with other students. The more I felt all of the dreadful things happening, the more I talked myself out of attending any college. We arrived at the admissions office. I walked to the receptionist to sign in. She looked like a freshman.

"I will let Ms. Turner know you're here. Would you like any tea or water?"

"No, I'm fine." I had no stomach for anything.

"Okay, please have a seat. Ms. Turner will be out shortly." My mom wrapped her arms around me and held my hand. She knew that when I got quiet my nerves were getting the best of me.

"It's okay, baby," Mom said. "God says, do you know the plans I have for you, plans to prosper you. To keep you in perfect peace. There is nothing to fear. I am here." Tears rolled down my face as my mom began whispering God's strength. I felt at peace and was ready to tackle the interview with confidence.

"Miss Johnson." Ms. Turner was everything I pictured her to be. Tall, long curly hair, manicured nails, grey business suit and stilettos. "It is such a pleasure to meet you. Mrs. Washington has told me so much about you. This must be your mother. Hello, please come in to my office." She shook my hand, there was a massive rock on her finger. We walked towards her office. The walls covered with positive quotes and phrases. Her desk was filled with family photos of her children and husband. It was very neat and in order.

"So, Miss Johnson, thank you for traveling to our wonderful school. I am so glad you have taken the time to visit. As I said, Mrs. Washington has told me a lot about you, and thinks very highly of you. What I would like to do during this meeting is tell you a little about the school and give you a tour with one of the students who will show you around campus while I go over your application and essay. How does that sound?"

"Sounds Good to me."

"Great! Well, to give you a little background, NYU was founded in 1831. It's the largest private university in the United States. I know that it may seem a little daunting, visiting such a large school, but trust me it gets very small once you learn to navigate and make friends. You will find that even the instructors care about the students success. You should never feel lost or behind in a class. Professors always offer to stay to give extra help for students. I am pleased to know that you did so well academically, and scored high on the SATs. Do you have any questions for me?"

"Well, I was wondering how soon would I know my acceptance?

"You will found out today. You were referred by my very good friend. Please let me know if you think of any additional questions. I want you to get the most out of your visit. In the meantime, I am going to let Tina, my receptionist, take you on your tour." Butterflies swarmed at jet speeds in my stomach. The more I thought about leaving my family, the more I wanted to stay at home forever. I got so used to my life back home. It was hard to think of anything different. Ms. Turner walked us out of her office, and introduced us to Tina, who was excited to give us a tour of the school.

"You are going to be happy here," she said. "This is my first year and I've already made so many friends. There are also so many things to do in the city. Let me show you around." My mom and I followed Tina out the building. The energy of the city was tangible. Students seemed focused, but also able to enjoy the college life. Our first stop was the dormitory.

"This is one of the dorms on campus. Coed. As you see, each room has a suite like feel, where you share a bathroom. There is also a lounge, computer lab, and study room for your convenience."

"Is there a curfew?"

"No, there isn't a curfew in any of the dorms." I could tell that didn't make my mom warm and fuzzy. As we walked out of the huge dormitory, Tina shared where most of her classes were held. She also explained she was from Los Angeles, studying film.

Her parents originally wanted her to go to medical school, but eventually accepted her dream of becoming a film director.

"Adjusting to NYU was a bit of a challenge. LA is a lot slower. Once I met friends to show me around, I quickly got used to city life."

"Tina, can you tell how us how big classes are?"

"Classes can range from fifty to eighty students, depending on the class. The great thing is, teachers are always available if you need further tutoring. Well, this is the cafeteria. The food is amazing." I studied students in the huge cafeteria, and thought about my tiny cafeteria in high school.

Our last stop was the recreation center. They all played pool, ping pong, or watched movies. There were a few restaurants inside, and a huge book store.

"A lot of my friends hang out here after class," she said. "There will be another orientation for freshman in the fall prior to classes. We can now head back to the admissions office."

Ms. Turner was ready to continue the meeting.

"Welcome back, I hope you enjoyed the tour. I had the opportunity to review your application, and job well done. I also shared your material with my colleagues, and we decided that we would love for you to join our NYU family." If my mom wasn't behind me I think I would have fainted. It all seemed unreal until now. I was finally going to be a college student. Through the tears all I could say was, "Yes, I would love to."

Traveling back to the airport, I thought about my life and what it would be like as a college student. My mom lectured the whole cab ride about boys and upper classmen plotting on freshman girls. She told me not to let boys in my dorm room, and remember how I was raised and to treat myself with respect. For the first time, I listened without any interruption. I knew my life would be different without her to go home to. I would soon be answering to myself, and the thought of being alone in a big city was very scary. But I knew deep down that I would be just fine.

CHAPTER 13

I was happy to be home, and even more about excited about Christmas and Reggie's party. With Christmas Eve the next day I had to do some last minute shopping, and more importantly get my outfit.

"Surprise!" My mom stood in the middle of the room with a present. "I know you have been anxious to go to the New Year's Eve party and you have been worried about what to wear. Well, I heard you talking to one of your friends on what you wanted to wear, so I went ahead and gave you a head start on your outfit." I tore opened the box, a pair of pink suede stilettos were laying inside so beautifully.

"Thank you so much mom! I love them. This makes my outfit so much easier."

"You deserve it. Tiffany is downstairs waiting. Enjoy your shopping day." I didn't want to tell Tiffany about my early Christmas gift, she always seemed to be so secretive about what she was wearing.

"Hey, Patrice! How was New York?" I swore this girl was hard of hearing.

"New York was great I was accepted," I said. There was confidence pushing my voice.

"Well, I will be at Georgetown. I can't wait until we visit each other over break."

"Yes, we will be finally on our own, no more high school and no more drama."

Instead of the mall, Tiffany took me to the outlets, to her favorite stores. I found a black suede dress that looked great with my hot pink pumps.

"Well, I have my outfit," said Tiffany. "Of course you won't see it until that night. I don't want you trying to copy." I busted out laughing. She always thought someone wanted to be just like her.

"You don't have to worry about a thing. I have my own identity." One thing I was taught was never let anyone think they can say anything they want to you. Always stand up for yourself by being direct.

"Girl, I am starving lets go to Chick-Fil-A."
We sat in the empty food court. Tiffany was going on and on about what I missed while visiting NYU.

"So, have you heard about Tracy? She is pregnant." I almost fell out of my chair and threw up all of my food.

"What!"

"Yes, she is. I couldn't believe it. She must be about three months. I saw her at a basketball game. She wasn't trying to hide it at all. Of course Mike was with her guiding her every step." I really couldn't believe what I was hearing. I wasn't sure if I was mad or sad.

"Wow, I thought she was going to leave him. She seemed so sad the last time we spoke, but I thought she would get the strength. Looking back, she was pregnant that entire time. I can't believe it."

"Well, believe it. She is soon to be a mother."
I couldn't sleep that night. All I could think of was the look of Tracy's face as I begged her to tell me why she was still with Mike. She was crying for help, yet stayed in a relationship because he said those three words I love you. Deep down she knew that Mike was unfaithful, and I warned her that this could happen. But it was too late. I wondered if Mike would still go off to college, or would he take off a year. So many thoughts swirled around in my head, so much that I fell asleep wondering why.

CHAPTER 14

—ɯ—

Christmas Eve at my house was always festive. At 10 a.m., Christmas carols were already blasting, and my mom and grandmother always made a big breakfast. I walked down stairs to most of my family, aunts, uncles, and little cousins running around. This was always my favorite time of year.

"Nice of you to join us sleepy head." The sound of that voice made me think I was dreaming. The only voice that I could trace that to was my father and I knew he was in Florida. Once I reached the bottom of the stairs there he was sitting on the couch drinking a cup of coffee.

"Daddy!" I ran into his arms and inhaled his cologne, the same smell I remembered as a little girl.

"Surprise, beautiful! You didn't think I was going to let you spend Christmas without your daddy did you. Besides, Desmond wanted to come to Florida, but I thought it would be best to come here and spend it with both of you." I was so happy I couldn't stop smiling, and couldn't wait to catch him up on my life.

Everyone finally reached the dining room table to feast on the biggest breakfast of the year. My grandmother started telling her stories of how Christmas was when she was a little girl. My grandfather watched, smiling at her with love. My father reminisced how he met my mother, and how proud he was of me and Desmond. Before they got around to talking about me, I was saved by the bell. I was shocked to see Tiffany, Lisa, and Amber walk in.

"Good Morning, everyone," Tiffany said.

"Hello, girls," my dad pulled out a couple of chairs. "We were just about to get started on Patrice and her upcoming college career. I assume all of you girls are going to college."

"Yes, sir."

"College was one of the best years of my life." My uncle Tony always went back to his college days. The best advice I can give your girls is stay in the books. The boys will always be around somewhere."

"Yes, the boys will always be there." My grandfather chimed in, the voice of wisdom. "Take this time in your life and really concentrate on being whole."

CHAPTER 15

———vn—

O nce the girls left that morning, I couldn't help, but think what they thought about that conversation. They expected to eat a feast. What they got was an interview. The thought of it made me laugh out loud. The remainder of the day, I helped my mom clean the house, and prepared for my dad to pick up me and my brother for dinner. I knew the restaurant would be a five star, so I wore a dress and heels. I still thought about Tracy a lot. I wanted so badly to call her, but it made me angry. I even thought about Kim, who I wished was still here. Going through this with her would be so much easier. I knew she would be reminding me about my value and not to worry about the past. She always had a way of making me feel special and constantly had me laughing about the silliest things. The thought of her made me to cry uncontrollably. I didn't know if anyone heard me.

"Patrice, Patrice, what's wrong? What happened? Why are you crying?" My brother was very protective over me and couldn't stand to see me upset.

"I was just thinking about Kim, that's all. I just miss her so much."

"Well, it's good to cry sometimes. You don't always have to be strong and cover up your emotions. I know you miss her. Kim was your best friend. Now, what you have to do is live your best life, knowing that she would want you to be happy."

"How did you get to be so smart?"

"Are you kidding me? I'm one of the smartest people you know." We both laughed and it was the first real laugh I had in a very long time.

My dad never disappointed when it came to restaurants.

We pulled up, and were greeted by a valet. They opened our doors and escorted us in the nicely dim dining area. There were huge glass tables with tropical fish swimming inside. I never saw anything like it. There was also a huge Christmas tree and a young lady playing the piano. As we were seated, we were immediately greeted by our waiter, who was very bubbly.

"Welcome to *El Filete*. Can I start you off with something to drink?"

"I want a Shirley Temple."

"I'll take a Coke," my brother said.

"And I'll take just water with lemon please."

"Wow dad, I thought you would order something else other than water."

"Can a man just have a glass of water without being questioned? You didn't hear me say anything about your Shirley temple. So, what's going on with both of you? Time is flying by so fast. What's new with you, Desmond?"

"Still, playing football trying to keep my grades up."

"That's good to hear, but let me correct you on one thing. You shouldn't be trying to keep your grades up, just simply do your best. You are very bright and will go far in life. Just continue to watch your circle, don't let too many people get too close to you. Always be mindful of who you call friend. And prepare for the future. Never get too complacent, continue to set goals and reach them. Can you promise that?"

"Yes."

"And you, Patrice, what's been new with you since you left Florida."

"Well, you will be glad to hear that I left Mike. The whole time he was seeing the girl Tracy. About a month ago she called me upset wanting to talk and shared how sorry she was and that she knew Mike cheated on her, but didn't have the strength to leave him. I even invited her to church and thought that she would break free. The other day I found out that she is pregnant. I just can't believe it."

"I'm proud of you for recognizing your worth and had the

courage to tell him that you deserve more. As far as this young lady she has her own decisions to make, and you can't consume yourself with her life. Mike should be a thing of the past. You should be able to see him and smile and say hello. Remember, always be able to give people their wings. God has something great for you and I can't wait to see what he has in store for both of you."

Talking, laughing, and eating steak and dessert left us all full and tired. After my dad dropped us off, I thought about his advice, about leaving Mike in the past and never looking back. Moving forward was now my only option, and wholeness is what I longed for.

CHAPTER 16

—ww—

The sun blazed through my window early Christmas morning. I remembered a time when I would be the first one waking my brother up to open all of our gifts. This time it was way past 10:00 a.m. and I could have slept for another hour. If it wasn't the smell of breakfast creeping its way to my room sleep would have won. Desmond must have had the Christmas bug, he had already opened all of his gifts. He got an Apple iPad, an iPhone, a gift card to iTunes, and clothes.

"Patrice, you almost slept Christmas away. Start opening up your gifts. Here this one is from dad." Dad had perfect timing because he just walked in. I tore open the pretty wrapping paper and I stared at an Apple iPad. I knew my brother wanted one, but didn't expect one of my own. "Thank you so much, daddy." The next gift was an Apple Computer.

"Now, I know that you need that for college. You will be doing a lot of papers. There is no excuse to bring home anything less than an A." My mom bought me a few pair of my favorite AG jeans, sweaters, camies, shoes, and Burberry perfume.

"Now where is my gift?" My mom and dad said at the same time.

"Mom, here is yours." She was like a five year old. Once she saw her Pandora bracelet she was in tears. Each charm was meaningful and she couldn't take her eyes off it.

"Thank you so much, Patrice. I love it." My brother bought her earrings and a shawl. Both my brother and I decided to go in together and get my dad a gift.

"Here you go, dad."

"Oh you shouldn't have."

"Wow, an iPod!"

"Yes, daddy, you're always complaining about not having one. Now you can download music before you leave and have something to listen to on the way back to Florida."

"Thank you so much. This means a lot. Very thoughtful."

"Well, breakfast is in the kitchen, help yourself. I'm going to stop by mom and dad's. I haven't heard from them. I'll be back shortly." I called Tiffany after breakfast to hear about her goodies.

"Hey, Tiffany, Merry Christmas."

"Hey, Patrice. Did you get everything you wanted?"

"I actually did, we usually don't get that much since we've gotten older."

"Same here. My dad bought me a Tiffany's bracelet and a pair of Joe Jeans and a couple of shirts. Do you have any plans tonight?"

"No, just spending time with the family. Before I forget, I would like to interview your dad for my class. The interview would be about what it means to be whole and having confidence as a young woman."

"Okay. I'll be sure to let him know. He will love that. You know how he likes to talk." All I could do was laugh, but I then thought Tiffany probably had no idea her dad had so much wisdom, and I wanted to soak it all in.

My mom didn't call and it was already in the middle of the afternoon. My dad had taken my brother to visit a few of his friends. I was home alone and called mom to see what she and my grandparents were doing.

"Patrice, honey I'm sorry I haven't called you," she said through tears."

"What! Mom, calm down. What's going on?"

"When I pulled up to the house there was an ambulance in the driveway taking Pop-Pop out of the house. Apparently, he hadn't been feeling good since last night and his blood pressure was sky high. I'm at the hospital right now. I think you should come."

"Okay, I'm on my way." I flew out of the house with the clothes on my back. My mind kept going back to Kim. I didn't know what I would do if I lost my grandfather. He seemed fine the other day. I parked in front of the ER and ran as fast as I could. I saw my mom with blood shot eyes, waiting with my grandmother.

"Is everything okay?"

"We don't know anything yet, sweetie," my grandmother said through tears. "We were just waiting for you. They moved him into Intensive Care. We can go back now." My grandfather had tubes in his nose and an IV plugged in his arm. I didn't know what to say. I walked towards his bed and brushed his hair back. Tears were flowing, and I didn't want to leave his side. As nurses came back to check his vital signs, we were instantly pushed out of the room. The doctor was paged and they were yelling code blue.

My grandmother fell into my arms crying hysterically.

"I'm sorry, but I'm going to have to ask you to leave. Please go to the waiting room. The doctor will be with you."

You could hear a pin drop as we sat in silence, seemed like time stopped.

"Ms. Johnson. Hello, I'm Dr. King. Your husband is fine. I know that was a scare for all of you. His blood pressure has dropped down to normal. His heart is also no longer beating at a rapid rate. He is now stabilized. I would like him to stay overnight so we can keep an eye on him."

"How did this happen?"

"Well, there is no way of telling how exactly it happened. But there are some things to avoid it happening again. Decrease his salt intake. Make sure he exercises his heart at least three times a day. Also, make a habit of checking his blood pressure. You saved his life. Well, ladies, I'm happy to give you a positive report. Please contact me directly if you have any additional questions." We went back to the room. He was knocked out sleeping. I wanted to wake him up and tell him to never to scare me like that again. I was ready to give him an earful, but so happy that my Pop-Pop was still with me. My biggest cheerleader.

CHAPTER 17

S itting in the hospital was exhausting. To my surprise, the clock showed 12 p.m. This was New Year's Eve and the party that I've been waiting for. I couldn't believe I slept so long, but felt refreshed and happy. My mom surprised me with a hair appointment at 2 p.m., and I didn't have to worry about my outfit.

"Well, hello sleepy head, I thought you were up by now."

"I tossed and turned all night worrying about Pop-Pop. I'm so glad he's okay."

"Yes, I was very scared. I don't know what I would do If I would lose him. Well, you know he's not going anywhere. He still has to see his baby walk across that stage and every other goal you accomplish in life." My mom held me tight, to let me know everything was going to be okay. I felt safe and never wanted to let go.

"You have to get ready for your hair appointment, and I have plans with my girlfriends tonight. Momma is going out on the town." We both laughed.

The hair salon was packed, but Tina always found a way to squeeze me in.

"Hi, Patrice! Come on back. Let's get you started. You know everyone is here for that party tonight. I know you are going since I heard Reggie has a crush on you." I spun my neck around so fast I thought I had whip lash.

"Where did you hear that?"

"Girl, please I work in a hair salon, people can't wait to tell me what they seen or heard."

"I don't know if he has a crush on me. We did go out once. He is so busy with basketball, and me with my school work...."

"Well, whatever the story is, you are a beautiful girl and you deserve the best. From what I hear, Reggie is a nice guy and comes from a great family, he's also extremely focused. You have no idea how many girls come in here talking about the star basketball player." I smiled, everything she said was true, but my mind wasn't on dating, but more on my future.

"So, enough about shop gossip, what are we doing with your hair? Let's do curls again. They always turn out great."

My hair turned out beautiful with bouncy curls. I went to the nail salon next door and got a manicure and pedicure. Hot pink polish to match my shoes. I prayed that the polish would last at least through the night. I was extremely clumsy. As I got my nails polished the nail tech was very friendly.

"So big New Year's Eve Party tonight, huh?"

"Yes, only a few more hours."

"That should be fun, we have been very busy today. I'm sure you already have your outfit picked out. Your hair looks beautiful."

"Thank you so much." I would get shy when people gave me compliments. God was showing me that I was worthy and beautiful both inside and out. Once my manicure and pedicure was finished, I walked at a snail pace to my car. I could've fainted when I saw Reggie's car parked next to mine.

"Hello, beautiful."

"Reggie, what are you doing here?"

"I had to stop at the grocery store to get snacks for tonight. I hope you're getting all fancy for my party and not going somewhere else." As I talked to Reggie I noticed girls in the hair salon pointing and shooting mean looks.

"Of course I will be there along with my crew."

"Good," he flashed his perfect smile. "I'll see you tonight."

"See you later." I thought he was the perfect gentleman.

I was extremely nervous. You would have thought that I was going to give a speech or walk down the aisle for my wedding. My hands were sweaty and my stomach was in knots.

"Patrice, your friends are here!"

"Send them upstairs!"

"Hey, Patrice, are you ready yet?" Tiffany always looked fabulous. She had on a black tube dress with red stilettos and red clutch bag. Her hair was pulled back in a bun with gold hoop earrings. Amber had on a black sequined shirt, jeans and black sequined stilettos. Her hair was long and flat ironed bone straight that fell passed her shoulders. Lisa had on a silver sequined tube top with black pants and silver sequined pumps. Her hair is naturally curly and was worn in big curls. I decided to wear a black suede dress and hot pink suede stilettos.

"You look hot, Patrice!" Tiffany was the loudest, but always that friend that made you feel great. "My dad is downstairs waiting for us. He refuses to let me drive on New Year's Eve."

"That's fine. Did you have a chance to ask him about me interviewing him?"

"No, I'm sorry I forgot, but you can ask him when we get in the car."

"You girls look great," my mom said. "Wait, let me grab my camera." We all huddled together and smiled and posed at least five times. "Now, you know these pictures are going on Facebook and Instagram."

"Not, until I approve," I chimed in. "You girls have a nice time. Patrice, I love you."

"I love you too, mom."

Once we hopped in the car, Tiffany's dad was happy to see all of us dressed up.

"You girls look stunning. These are some of the happiest days of your lives. Enjoy them. How have you been doing, Patrice?"

"I'm doing fine Mr. Clark. I have a school project that is due after break and I wanted to know if I could interview you. Since I have been hearing so much about wholeness, I wanted to get your feedback on dating and wholeness from a man's point of view. Would you be available to do it?"

"I would love to. Just give me the time and place. I think that is an excellent idea."

"Great! How about Monday afternoon? I can come by your house and we can have the interview where Bible Study was held."

"Sounds good to me."

"Thanks, Mr. Clark."

"Well, girls we have arrived. I will be back to pick you up at 2 a.m. Have a nice time and Happy New Year."

"Happy New Year," We all said in unison.

Reggie's parents greeted us as we walked in the house. This was our first time seeing his parents, and we all immediately noticed the resemblance. His dad was very tall and distinguished. His mom was beautiful and had gorgeous flowing hair, and a great smile.

"Hi, girls, welcome. Please proceed downstairs where there is plenty of food."

"Have a nice time girls," his dad said with a deep voice. Walking down stairs the lights were dim and the DJ already had everyone dancing. Reggie's aunt was making sure everyone was comfortable and took our coats.

"Hello, girls. I remember you from the last party. Don't be shy, food is over there in the corner, and soda and juice is in the cooler. Reggie is around here somewhere. Have a nice time." Drake blared through the speakers, Tiffany, Amber, Lisa and I all jumped up to our favorite song. I must have been in a zone because Mike was right in front of me when I looked up. I didn't see him coming.

"Patrice, you look hot."

"Thanks, Mike. How are you?" For some reason, it felt like I was talking to a stranger, and in a lot of ways he was."

"I've been good. Busy with basketball. I got into Syracuse. So I'm super excited about that."

"Wow, that's huge. Congratulations!" I screamed over blaring music.

"Thanks! I hear you're going to NYU, that's great!"

"Thanks! I can't wait!"

"Well, it was nice talking to you. Happy New Year." The look on his face was like a deer in head lights. He must have thought that things would be like old times. I was taught to never look back.

As I danced with my girls, song after song, we were each approached by guys who were holding up the wall.

"Do you girls want to dance? Or do you want to dance with each other all night?" We all looked at each other and gave the non-verbal I don't care. The guy I danced with was from the football team. He was one of the star players, but seemed to be very shy off the football field. For some reason he was outgoing and the life of the party.

"So, your name is Patrice, right?"

"Yeah!"

"My name is Shawn! I see you a lot between classes, but never got the nerve to come up to you."

"Awwww...it's nice to meet you."

"Me and a couple of friends are going out for breakfast after this, you girls are welcomed if you want."

"Thanks for the invite but we have other plans." The funny thing was, the only plans we had were with our beds.

Walking upstairs to cool off I heard Reggie's voice. "Are you leaving already?"

"Hey, Reggie, no I just wanted to freshen up. It is a sweat box down there."

"Well, you can sit up here for a while where it's cool. I seldom get to enjoy my own party, I'm always so busy entertaining. I'm glad that you came out though. For some reason, when I'm around you, I feel very calm and at peace. It's not too often that I meet people like you."

"Thanks Reggie, that's very nice to say. I think we better stop talking before one of these girls scratch my eyes out."

"I won't have any of that in here, besides you should not be worried about any of these girls. I know what they see, star basketball player, possible NBA draft. My dad has prepared me for this since I was born. You're different from all of the rest. Like I said, you have a peace about you. And you seem to have a good idea of who you are. You also seem very focused and driven. I like the way you demand respect. You could have stayed with Mike while he cheated on you and deny the truth. You chose to leave because you know your worth. I like that."

"Thank you for saying that. I have a great support system and I'm learning more and more about myself every day."

"I know that we both have too much going on to even con-sider a relationship. I mean, we're both going away to college. I will be crazy busy with basketball. But I want you to know that I've seriously thought about approaching you as someone I would like to get to know better. But I want to do it the right way when the time is right. I do have a question though?" My stomach did back flips waiting for what he would say next. "Will you go to the prom with me?" I could've fainted right there in the kitchen. I didn't give the prom that much thought. I planned to go with my girls like ev-eryone else had been doing.

"Yes, I would love to." Reggie's mom came in the kitchen and rushed us out to tell us the New Year's count-down was begin-ning. We heard the screams in the other room. Once I found my crew we all held each other's hands tight as we watched the big countdown on the big screen.

"TEN, NINE, EIGHT, SEVEN, SIX, FIVE, FOUR, THREE, TWO, ONE!!!! Happy New Year!!!!!" There was a lot of love in the room, everyone hugged folks they really didn't know. The DJ continued playing the music and I noticed Reggie from across the room smiling from ear to ear. I couldn't wait to tell my girls that we were going to the prom.

CHAPTER 18

—ᴍ—

I decided to stay at Tiffany's house after the party. I was glad that Amber and Lisa also agreed to have a sleep over. We stayed up all night talking about who was dancing with who and who had on what.

"Somebody was missing before the ball dropped. Where did you disappear off to? Talking to Reggie?" Amber loved making a big deal out of nothing.

"Yes, nosey, I was talking to Reggie."

"So, what did he say? Is that your new boyfriend?"

"No, Oprah, he's not my boyfriend. We're just friends, but he did ask me to the prom."

"Oh my gosh! He did! What are you going to wear!?" Tiffany was more excited than me.

"I don't know. It's all happening so fast." Tiffany jumped in before I can finish my next sentence.

"Well, you have to figure it out. The prom will be here before you know it. Now, that makes me want to at least have a prom date." With all the excitement Tiffany, Lisa, and Amber were fast asleep and I soon dozed off thinking about my perfect night.

"Hi, party animals, breakfast is ready when you decide to get up. I have to run a few errands. Tiffany your dad is in his office if you need him." Tiffany's mom was the sweetest lady. She always had on a smile on her face and bent over backwards for Tiffany.

"Thanks, mom."

"Tiffany, since I'm here, do you think I can borrow one of your outfits so I can interview your dad. I may as well get it done now."

"Sure, pick out anything in my closet you need. I'll go let

him know in case he leaves." I put on something professional for the camera, black blazer, white button up shirt, and black skirt.

"He said he would love to. Come down to the office when you're ready."

"Cool." I jotted down a few questions and prayed that it came out perfectly so I could ace this last assignment.

Once I scarfed down pancakes and bacon, I walked the long corridor to Mr. Clark's office.

"Patrice, good morning. Did you girls have a nice time?"

"Yes, we had a lot of fun."

"I'm glad to hear it."

"Well, you tell me where to sit. Tiffany brought the video camera and it's ready to go."

"Okay. And just to remind you, this interview will be about wholeness and what you would tell girls my age about dating and relationships."

"Great. I have a lot to say on that topic fortunately, having a teenage daughter. Whenever you're ready." As we both took our seats I jumped right in.

"Alright my first question is: a lot of young girls my age aren't fortunate enough to have a father figure. Because of that they are looking for love through boys. What advice would you give that girl?"

"I would tell that girl that no one will ever love her more than God. It is through His love that she will learn her value and worth. The only way to know what true love means is through a personal relationship with God. Just because a boy says the magic words I love you doesn't mean it's true. You see, love is an action, not just words. Young girls have to be careful when they hear those words, a lot of the time young boys are trying to get something from you and once they get it, they're on to the next young girl. Love also isn't supposed to hurt. It feels really good. You should never have to guess about a person's love for you. 'Love is patient. Love is kind.' You should bask in this person's presence and feel a peace. More importantly, when God sends a young woman a man, it will be a reflection of God's perfect love. Now that's powerful."

"How would someone recognize that kind of love?"

"Oh, you will know it. It's just like trying on a pair of shoes. It will just fit. It won't be a mystery. The God of the universe takes care of the birds in the air. Surely He will take care of His creation that was created in His image. The worst thing young girls can do is search for love in someone else, that is where you will get hurt. Love isn't a feeling. Love is a choice. Love takes work and sacrifice. Feelings change like the weather. When that feeling is gone, so are they, too. The person who loves you is in it for the long haul. But before you can love someone else, you must love yourself first. You must go through the process from a caterpillar to a beautiful butterfly so you can fly in wholeness and in love." Tears ran down my face with his last statement. I didn't think this interview would touch me the way it did. I wanted every young girl to hear this because I knew many were struggling in the same area.

"Thank you so much, Mr. Clark."

"You are quite welcome, Patrice. Anytime. This is such a great topic that you chose, and I hope it will touch young girls and provoke them to love themselves first."

CHAPTER 19

The rest of the weekend flew by, and school was back in session. Graduation was soon approaching. I still had to get my dress for prom. I was so excited! My brother and I rode together and he couldn't stop talking about the holiday weekend with our dad. The parking lot seemed like everyone was still floating from Christmas break. All of the seniors were definitely happy, there was only a few months to go. With my tape in hand, I went straight to my broadcasting class to turn in my last assignment.

"Well, hello, Miss Patrice, I hope you enjoyed your Christmas holiday. You are the first to turn in your assignment. I hope this is an A.

"I'm sure it will be."

"You have done very well this year. I was told by Mrs. Washington that you're going to NYU. That is great! I hope to see you on T.V. one day, young lady.

"Thanks, Ms. Smith, I hope so."

Classes were a breeze for the rest of the day. My last class was dismissed early, and I ran into Tracy walking to my car. She looked to be nine months pregnant.

"Tracy."

"Oh, hi, Patrice." She looked great and had a special glow about her. She was smiling from ear to ear.

"How are you? Are you excited to finally be leaving high school?"

"Yeah, I can't wait. I really can't wait to have this baby. He kicks me all night."

"Cool, you're having a boy. He is going to be so adorable."

"I want to thank you for our talks. You really encouraged

me to be strong. You're also the reason that I joined church. My mom and I go every Sunday. You will also be surprised to know that I left Mike. He will be in our child's life, but it was time for me to stand on my own and not be so dependent on a relationship. I will start classes in the fall at the University. I have a great support system."

"That's great Tracy. I'm glad that you chose what is best for you. You look amazing. You will be a wonderful mom."

"Thanks again, Patrice. Call me sometime."

"I will. Congratulations again."

—⁕—

Finally, the last day of classes, and my TV production class was airing our projects for the whole school to see. When my assignment popped up on the monitor, I wanted the floor to swallow me whole. I was so nervous about what people would say and wondered if anyone would like my interview topic or even pay attention. As I scanned the room, the guys and girls were glued to the screen. I saw some girls wiping away tears, and guys listening to Mr. Clark's every word. After class, my teacher hugged me so tight I could barely breathe.

"Patrice, that was a wonderful interview. The students were all moved by the topic. You found a way to bring in both audiences. Job well done." Job well done translates into A+. Go me!

—⁕—

CHAPTER 20

—⚍—

Prom and graduation were weeks away, and my mom was taking me shopping for my fabulous dress. Reggie decided to wear a white suite. I had no idea what I was going to wear, and I was freaking out. Reggie said that his friends didn't have dates so they would go with my crew. He also planned to have a Range Rover limo pick us up. It would be a night I wouldn't forget.

My grandmother came with my mom and me to shop at one of the boutiques. As soon as I walked in, I loved all of the dresses on the rack. The sales lady was very helpful and opened a dressing room for me. My grandmother didn't love the dresses, she wanted me to look like Cinderella on my prom night. When I came out in my first dress, I didn't get much excitement. The dress was a long red halter fit with embellishment around the waist. My mom was the first to chime in.

"I don't like that dress at all. It doesn't seem like it fits well. Try on that gold dress that we love."

"I agree with your mother. That Is not the dress." You would have thought I was picking out my wedding dress. The gold sequenced dress fit perfectly. It was one shoulder and fell just below my calves. I had to have great shoes. When I made my entrance I heard gasps.

"Patrice, that is the dress. You look so beautiful."

"Awwww, don't cry, Grandmom."

"I just can't help it. You look like a princess."

"You look spectacular. There is no need to look for another dress. This is it." I was glad that the boutique also had an amazing shoe department. It didn't take me long to find the shoes that fit perfectly. They were gold sequenced peep-toe pumps. Dress and shoe picking was done. I was ready for prom.

My mom planned to throw a huge party for prom and graduation, only days away. The crew and I planned to go to Miami for senior week, and I knew my dad would roll out the red carpet. This would be the last time before college that we would all be together, and I couldn't wait! Things were going great, and I felt very good about myself. I felt like I could be anyone I wanted and there was nothing that was going to hold me back. My mom reminded me to open some mail that I had been neglecting. One of the envelopes read PLEASE DON'T DISCARD in red letters, it was from Mrs. Washington. I tore it open. It stated:

Dear Ms. Patrice Johnson,

It will be an honor for you to speak at the high school graduation. You are a shining example that whatever you put your mind to you can succeed. I understand this year was tough with the death of your close friend, but through perseverance and faith you are still standing. I am so very proud of you and wish you continued success at my alma mater, NYU. I know you will soar and never stop dreaming.

Sincerely,

Mrs. Carol Washington

Knots formed in my stomach and I thought that I would faint.

"Patrice, are you alright? It looks like you've seen a ghost."

"Mom, I've been just asked to speak at the high school graduation. I have no idea what I will say. I don't have a speech prepared. Should I write something? What am I going to do?"

"That is a huge compliment to get selected amongst your peers. Just speak from your heart. You will be fine."

That whole day I was a nervous wreck. I never would have guessed in a million years that I would be asked to speak in front of the whole senior class. I tried sitting down, and writing something either funny or serious. Should it be entertaining in the beginning or the end? My mind was all over the place. As I sat there, not knowing what to do, I decided to take my mom's advice and be me: Patrice. That's what Kim would have wanted.

CHAPTER 21

It was the day of the prom, and I was finishing up some last minute errands. Reggie's dad was handling the car, and he would also be our driver for the night. Tiffany, Amber, and Lisa were going to leave from my house. After prom, Reggie's dad offered to take us out for a midnight breakfast. I drove to my hair appointment, and thought a lot about my high school year and how proud I was of myself. I learned a lot about who I was, and loved myself so much more. I was thankful for my family and friends, and how I didn't give up after my best friend died. I respected myself enough to end a relationship with someone who wasn't respecting me.

I was the first one at the hair salon, and Tina was unbelievably bubbly this time of day.

"Patrice! Hey, girl, I know you can't wait until prom and graduation."

"No, I can't wait. I want to have my hair in a lose bun today."

"Nice, great choice. Let's get your hair washed so I can create this masterpiece."

Once my hair was washed and blow dried, Tina didn't waste time talking about who was going to prom.

"So, I hear that you're going to prom with Mr. Reggie."

"I am. His friends are going with my friends as dates."

"Wow, you guys are going to have a blast. I didn't go to my prom. Back then I didn't feel that good about myself. I always admire girls who get to experience that."

"I'm sorry to hear that."

"That was a long time ago. It took time for me to love myself. I'm happy to see that you carry yourself with confidence. You will definitely go far." I didn't always feel that way. It was a time that I looked confident, but this time I was feeling that way too.

After my hair was done, I made a dash for the nail salon next door before the rush came and got a French manicure and pedicure. This was the last of my errands, and I had the rest of the day to relax.

"Wow, your hair looks great!" The owner was always very nice.

"Thank you."

"We will be very busy today. You were very smart to get in and out."

"Yes, I couldn't be late for the big day."

"So what college are you going to?"

"I'm going to NYU."

"Very smart girl. Don't forget to come by and visit between college breaks. I know that you will be very successful."

"Thanks." I was feeling like a million bucks and all I had to do was rest. We all decided to leave for prom by 5 p.m., and I refused to be late.

CHAPTER 22

—ᴍ—

Five o'clock was fast approaching. I was making great time getting ready. Once I showered, my mom helped me with my dress. My loose bun was in tact, and I broke my shoes in by walking around the house. My mom surprised me with her beautiful clutch bag.

"I know you thought that you would end up taking one of your bags. But when I saw this dress I instantly thought of my bag. It matches perfectly."

"Mom, it's beautiful. I have never seen this bag before."

"Well, you haven't seen all my things."

"I guess you're right."

"Thank you so much. I love it."

"You're so welcome. Cherish every moment tonight. It goes fast. You look so beautiful. So I am about to cry. So hurry up. Your friends are down stairs waiting, and Reggie and his dad just pulled up." I was nervous to make my grand entrance. For the first time, I looked at myself and saw a beautiful young woman before me. I not only looked beautiful, I felt beautiful.

As all of my friends gathered outside for pictures, the neighbors all came out and watched us like we were celebrities. We all looked at each camera listening to screams of people with the cameras trying to give us direction. They reminded me of the paparazzi.

"Well, I think it's time to hit the road," Reggie's dad said. Tiffany, Amber, and Lisa were all happy with their dates. They each looked amazing with their dresses, hair and makeup. Tiffany decided to wear a long turquoise blue dress with silver stilettos. Amber had a beautiful yellow dress embellished with bling at the top and flowed long at the bottom. Lisa wore a beautiful purple tube dress knee length, and strapped black stilettos. Reggie's friends complimented each one of my friends. I was glad that we were together. The limo was ready. Reggie's dad was cool and played our favorite songs.

"I'm happy that I'm going to prom. I didn't really plan on going since I was working so hard this year with the team. My dad really pushed me to go, and I knew exactly the girl to ask." All eyes were on me with that last statement. All I could do was smile.

"We are going to have so much fun tonight. No more school work, no more tests, this is truly going to be a celebration," Reggie's friend chimed in.

Prom was held in a beautiful hotel downtown. People were waiting in lines to get in. Everyone looked so different dressed up. I barely recognized anyone. Reggie was the perfect gentleman holding my hand. I noticed the stares from the other girls. I smiled and nodded. I was truly here to have a great time.

The inside was decorated beautifully with ice sculptures, a dance floor that looked like it was made of glass, and hundreds of balloons in our school colors, yellow and blue. The photographer was already taking pictures. My crew didn't waste time hitting the dance floor with their dates. I followed and grabbed Reggie by the hand.

Before I sweated my hair out, I asked Reggie and the rest of the crew to get our pictures taken. Waiting in line, I noticed Mike standing wearing a black suit. As soon as we had eye contact, he wasted no time making his way over to start conversation.

"Patrice, is that you? I barely recognized you. You look great!"

"Thank you, Mike."

"Oh, so I can't get a hug or anything. Okay, okay. I get it. I don't mean any disrespect. You do look very beautiful. It's like you have this special glow about you. I can't explain it. Well, I don't want to interrupt your night." I was so happy that he finally walked away. It felt good that he saw me at my best, confident and secure in my own skin.

After our pictures, we hit the dance floor. I couldn't stop smiling. Before midnight, the prom king and queen were announced, football player and cheerleader. No one was surprised. They were the perfect couple and liked by the whole school. Reggie's dad was outside waiting and none of us wanted the night to end.

We all agreed to go to IHOP for a late night breakfast. The lobby was jam packed. Luckily, Reggie's dad was thinking ahead and had made a reservation. We were seated right away.

"That was a hot party," Tiffany said. "I haven't danced all night like that in years."

"Yes, I definitely agree with that," Amber said with a yawn. "Can you believe that we will be graduating in a few weeks?"

"Where did the time go? It seems like we were just in the ninth grade yesterday." We all burst out laughing. Reggie always had everybody in stitches.

"Time did fly by. I've been so much in a rush to graduate that sometimes I want time to slow down just a little bit." I wasn't sure if I should share that I would be giving the commencement speech. I also didn't want it to be a surprise when I walked on that stage. Since these were my closest friends. I had I decided to just blurt it out.

"I'm giving the commencement speech." Amber almost spit out her food. Tiffany looked at me like she saw a ghost, and Lisa was so busy eating I don't think she heard a word I said.

"Really, that is huge!" Reggie was the only one able to say anything in that moment.

"Thank You."

"Wow, Patrice that is great!" It was funny to see it finally marinate with Tiffany. "When did you find out?"

"Mrs. Washington sent me a letter in the mail a few weeks ago. I am still so shocked. I really don't have anything prepared, I'm just going to speak from the heart. I am nervous."

"Don't be," Reggie said with a comforting voice. "We will all be there to cheer you on. Besides, think of it this way, Mrs. Washington wouldn't have asked you if you couldn't do it. You got this!"

"I hope so, or it's me standing up there with stage fright. If that happens all of y'all better come to my rescue and get me out of there."

"If you do that I'm taking over and you know how I like to talk." Just thinking of Tiffany giving the speech was funny. She talked loud and would go and on and on.

"Seriously, thanks for all of your support, and like Reggie said, I got this."

Graduation was only a few days away, and my cap and gown were hanging in the closet. My dad was in town, and my mom was preparing for a family party. I was still nervous about my upcoming speech, but knew that everything would turn out just fine. I couldn't stop thinking about prom, and how Reggie treated me like a princess. I hoped that we would keep in touch while in college. He definitely had a bright future ahead. We both decided that we would remain friends. Starting a relationship wasn't the right thing to do. This was the time to remain focused.

"Is the graduate ready for her speaking engagement?"

"Dad! I didn't' know you were downstairs."

"Your mother told me that you didn't write anything. She's right, speak from your heart. You will be more relatable that way. All of your peers will be able to relate to your experiences. God is preparing you for something great."

"I finally feel that. I'm unsure what that is. I was so shocked when I got that letter. I would have thought the class president would have been chosen, not me."

"You see, you're learning a lesson, that God uses ordinary people to do extraordinary things. I am sure you will inspire many today. You have a huge testimony. I see that your prom pictures came in. You look stunning. Who was your prom date?"

"His name is Reggie, and he's on the basketball team. He comes from a great family. His focus is on education and basketball right now. We both agreed that it's too early for a relationship."

"Well, this young man sounds like he has his head on straight. Timing is everything and relationships are something you never have to chase. God's timing is always perfect. The timing isn't for a relationship but it is time to graduate. Congratulations, baby. Daddy is so very proud of you."

CHAPTER 23

—ᏗᏗ—

It was the day of graduation and I was surprisingly calm. My mom made breakfast, and for the rest of the day I relaxed while my mom coordinated the party for later. I heard my grandparents and all of my cousins laughing and listening to music downstairs. My brother came in and out of my room to check if I was still breathing. My focus was only on the speech. As I lay on my bed with my eyes closed, I could hear my door opening slowly.

"Patrice, darling are you sleeping?"

"No, grandma I'm just resting. I'm feeling a little jittery. I don't know what to do with myself right now." We both laughed. She sat on my bed scanning the room. She looked at me like only a grandmother could.

"I remember when you first came from the hospital. You were the most beautiful baby I had ever seen. I remember setting up your crib in this room. You were also the baby that could cry all day long." I had to laugh because I was still a cry baby at times.

"Now, look at you. You have grown up into this beautiful, classy, confident, young lady that has conquered rejection and still studied hard in school when losing her best friend. Not too many adults could have handled that. You have endurance that many admire. That's why you were chosen to speak in front of an audience. I heard that you haven't written anything, so I am so excited what God gives you to speak. Remember that you are beautifully and wonderfully made in secret, and you can conquer all through a God that lives on the inside of you." As my grandmother stroked my hair, tears fell. I heard the door shut behind her. With her encouraging words, I felt strong and couldn't wait to deliver my speech.

The parking lot was packed and there were police directing

traffic. My family went to find their seats outside while I looked for Mrs. Washington. It was so nice to see everyone in there blue cap and gowns. I wanted so badly to see my crew, but I knew they were probably already seated. Mrs. Washington's was in her office speaking to another student.

"Patrice, you look so beautiful. Are you ready to get up there soon?"

"Yes, I didn't have a program so I wasn't sure when I would go up."

"Well, after I give the welcome you are going to be next." I felt my knees buckle and thought my legs would run away without me.

"Really?"

"Yes, young lady. So we have to get out there now. We don't want to keep people waiting. It's a hot one today." I followed Mrs. Washington outside to the sea of people--it must have been thousands. I couldn't believe they would all see me on stage in a few minutes. I saw my mom, dad, brother, and grandparents sitting in the audience. I also noticed Tiffany, Amber, and Lisa along with Reggie and his friends. We all locked eyes, and they all smiled with a *you're going to do great* look. As I took my seat on stage, Mrs. Washington approached the microphone and greeted the graduates.

"Greetings, Class of 2014. This is your day. You have made it to the finish line!" The crowd screamed and waved their caps in the air. "Each one of you should be very proud of yourselves. Not many made it to where you sitting today. You are here because you believed in yourself. Congratulations! To give your commencement speech I have chosen one of your classmates. One who has shown true resilience in the face of turmoil. She had the confidence during times of weakness. Please help me welcome Patrice Johnson!" My hands felt like they were dripping with water and I thought I would faint as I was carried by only God to the podium. I opened my mouth:

"Thank you Mrs. Washington. WE DID IT!!! I am so happy for all of us. There were moments during this journey that I thought I would never make it to this day. I am so thankful to have a huge support system, my mom, dad, grandmom and grandfather. My friends. I am a living witness that trials come to make you stronger, and push you to something greater than yourself. We are all winners, born to succeed our wildest dreams. I know this is a time of celebration, but after this there is still work to be done. Some will go off to college, while others will go immediately into the work force. Regardless of what we choose to do, we all must continue to push ourselves. We have to continue to use the tools our family has instilled in us; and what our teachers have taught us. There is still work to be done. All of the tests, papers, and more tests and papers; were all preparing us for the real world that is waiting for all of us. Everything that we complained about has shaped us into strong, confident, bright young men and women. We are all conquerors. We all lost a beautiful soul, my friend Kim. She looked so forward to this day. She looked forward to going off to college. None of these things would ever come into fruition for her. So starting this day, in memory of Kim, let's decide to live life, not with fear, but with courage. I am excited to see what we will become. We have been prepared for greatness! Let's all exceed expectations starting today! CONGRATULATIONS!"

"Thank you, Patrice. Now, that's what I call a speech. Yes, you are all conquerors. Go and show the world what you got!" I was so relieved to be done with the speech. Now I can relax without worrying about fainting all day. After I walked the stage and received my diploma, I cheered for all of my favorite girls. The crowd screamed when Reggie's name was called. I was also proud to see Mike receive his diploma. As Tracy walked across the stage, I screamed and clapped for her. I was so happy that she was walking in confidence and not hanging on to someone that was tearing her down. Once the whole class received diplomas, the crowds dispersed. Everyone was taking pictures and balloons filled the air. I took so many pictures with my family and friends. My dad gave me two dozen red roses. As I said my goodbyes to classmates, we promised to stay in touch. I felt a tap on my shoulder from behind.

"Mrs. Washington." She hugged me so tight.

"Patrice, you did absolutely amazing. I knew you had star power. You really inspired many. I can't wait to see you spread your wings. Please call me once you get settled at NYU. And if you don't call me, I will call you." We both laughed.

"I promise, Mrs. Washington. You have inspired me to do great things."

My house was packed with so many people, some I didn't even recognize. My mom must have invited the whole neighborhood, or maybe people invited themselves. The food was that good.

I opened the door everyone screamed, *"CONGRATULATIONS,"* and balloons floated around the whole house. It was nice seeing family. Everyone complimented me on the speech and said there wasn't a dry eye out there. I was happy I didn't see any tears from the podium or I would have been crying, too. I ate as much as I could stomach, laughed, and cried tears of joy with my family. This was the day that I had been waiting for, and I was surrounded by love. Tomorrow I would be on the plane with the crew to Miami for senior week. The celebration would continue.

CHAPTER 24

—◊◊◊—

I had a 12 p.m. flight, and my dad was packed and ready to go. I packed very light since most of our time would be spent at the beach. The girls would meet us at the gate. My mom hated to see me leave so soon, but understood that senior week happened after graduation, and besides, I deserved this vacation.

"Patrice, call me as soon as you get there."

"Okay."

"Also, call your grandparents, you know how they worry. "

"I will."

"Alright, honey. I love you. Enjoy yourself down there with your friends."

"I love you too, mom." My dad got to the airport in a blink of an eye. He always drove like a speed racer. The airport seemed pretty empty. Once we went through security, I saw the girls waiting at the gate.

"Miami here we come!" I said it as loud as Tiffany would. We all ran and hugged each other as if we hadn't seen each other in years.

"I can't wait to lay on the beach and relax. We are going to have so much fun!"

"Okay, does everybody have their iPods?" I sounded like my mother.

"Of course, music is on deck." Lisa said with excitement.

"Did you speak with Reggie before you left?" Tiffany asked.

"Yeah, he stopped by my house to wish me a safe trip."

"He's very sweet."

"I can't wait to see your dad's house. And since he lives

walking distance from the beach, you know that's where I'll be. And we have to go jet skiing." Lisa was so excited I thought she would burst.

"Delta flight # 5736 I will call you by zone number." We fell into line, filed in on the plane, and settled in our seats. My dad was offered a seat in first class due to his frequent flyer miles. Once we were all comfortable in our seats, we all plugged in our iPods and fell fast asleep.

CHAPTER 25

—⚍—

The pilot announced our landing. It felt like I just closed my eyes. Watching the girls light up as they scanned the beautiful city was like watching them open up gifts. Once we were off the plane, we caught a shuttle to my dad's car, and arrived at his place.

"Welcome to Miami, girls. I am sure you will have a blast here. There is a lot to do, and I am here as your personal taxi to show you around. I do live across the street from the beach, and all of the great restaurants. Patrice, has been here enough times, and will show you around as well. You can all hit the beach first and after that I can take you all out for dinner at one of my favorite restaurants." My dad grabbed all of the luggage, and showed the girls around the house. I followed as they watched in awe of the décor.

"This house is so beautiful," said Amber. "I don't ever want to leave."

"Well if you don't want to leave, you're going to have to start paying some bills." We all laughed. "Each one of you will have your own room and bathroom. If you girls need anything, please let me know. Patrice knows where everything is. I'm going to go relax and get unpacked. Have fun at the beach ladies." We didn't waste any time getting changed. At the beach we rented beach chairs and umbrellas, and stared at the ocean.

"I can't believe we are here. This is so amazing." Tiffany said.

"Yes, ladies in a few months we will all be in college." Amber was right. In a few months we would be all so far apart from each other. We would all have to start over making new friends.

"We have to promise," I said, making sure I had everyone's

attention. "That we call each other as much as we can." Tiffany choked up as I spoke.

"And we also have to promise that we encourage eachother when times get hard," Lisa chimed in.

"Lastly, we have to promise that we can make each one of our dreams come true." We all yelled promise in unison through tears. I laid back on my beach chair and stared at God's creation. I promised Him and myself that I was ready for college, and that I would succeed. Finally, I felt whole.

REFLECTIONS

1. Why was it so difficult for Patrice to believe Mike cheated on her with Tracy? Would you believe your friend if she told you?

_____

_____

_____

_____

_____

_____

_____

_____

2. If you found out your boyfriend was disloyal, then would you stay? Would you try to work it out?

_____

_____

_____

_____

_____

_____

_____

3. Do you ever wonder why you were born? Do you ever wonder about your purpose? What do you dream about doing? Write it out.

_____

_____

_____

_____

_____

_____

4. Do you feel confident on the inside? Do you ever compare yourself to other girls? If so why?

_____

_____

_____

_____

_____

_____

_____

_____

5. God says that you are fearfully and wonderfully made. Write all of the beautiful things about yourself.

_____

_____

_____

_____

_____

_____

_____

6. Has this book helped you with your confidence? If so how?

_____

_____

_____

_____

_____

7. Will you recommend this book to a friend?

_____

_____

_____

_____